EUROPE AT BAY

In the Shadow of US Hegemony

Alan W. Cafruny
J. Magnus Ryner

LYNNE
RIENNER
PUBLISHERS

BOULDER
LONDON

Published in the United States of America in 2007 by
Lynne Rienner Publishers, Inc.
1800 30th Street, Boulder, Colorado 80301
www.rienner.com

and in the United Kingdom by
Lynne Rienner Publishers, Inc.
3 Henrietta Street, Covent Garden, London WC2E 8LU

Library of Congress Cataloging-in-Publication Data
Cafruny, Alan W.
    Europe at bay: in the shadow of US hegemony / Alan W. Cafruny
& J. Magnus Ryner.
    Includes bibliographical references and index.
    ISBN 978-1-58826-513-5 (hardcover : alk. paper)
    ISBN 978-1-58826-537-1 (pbk. : alk. paper)
    1. European Union. 2. International relations. I. Ryner, J. Magnus.
II. Title.
JN30.C34 2007
341.242'2—dc22   2007008737

British Cataloguing in Publication Data
A Cataloguing in Publication record for this book
is available from the British Library.

Printed and bound in the United States of America

    The paper used in this publication meets the requirements
∞ of the American National Standard for Permanence of
    Paper for Printed Library Materials Z39.48-1992.

    5 4 3 2 1

Contents

Preface

THE PUBLICATION OF THIS BOOK represents the culmination of eight years of part-time collaboration and coauthorship. The first product of that collaboration was our coedited anthology, *A Ruined Fortress? Neoliberal Hegemony and Transformation in Europe*. The chief objective of *A Ruined Fortress?* was to introduce to the analysis of the European Union, in a sustained way, insights and concepts of the "new" critical international political economy (e.g., Murphy and Tooze, 1991) that progressively has established itself as an approach to international studies over the past two decades. The chief objective of the current book is different, as it seeks to address a gap in the literature.

One does not have to search far for short, sharp statements about the EU as a prospective superpower, a space of economic prosperity, or indeed a haven of civilization, written broadly from both liberal and conservative perspectives. The consensus view coming out of this literature is that, if only enlightened European elites could overcome petty squabbles and overly pampered welfare state constituencies, then—to the comfort of some, and the fear of others—a "new European century" is not unlikely. Equally, one does not have to go far to find a similar literature written from a broadly disillusioned "third way," center-left perspective. Recognizing the EU in its present form as the only game in town, this literature now generally agrees with the liberal and conservative perspectives, but holds out the hope that a leaner version of Europe's social model will not only persist, but also constitute a beacon to the world.

There are few books, however, at least in English, that are written from a perspective that intellectually defends the instincts of many ordinary Europeans who recently have made their voices heard in popular mobilizations, referenda, and protest votes. This is an instinct that insists that there is still something rational not only in *liberté*, but also in *égalité* and *fraternité* (solidarity), as cherished and indivisible norms of European political enlightenment. From such a position, welfare state arrangements do not seem anachronistic, but rather remain necessary for the good life—and, indeed, for civilization. Insofar as these arrangements are in crisis, this is due to the powers that be. We believe that insights from critical international political economy validate this instinct: Europe's problems are not primarily a result of dysfunctions in the social model, but due rather to a complex set of structural power relations, captured by the term "US (minimal) hegemony," that are in part enacted and reproduced through EU networks as presently configured. Our objective in this book, then, is to provide a succinct, clear, and reasonably accessible account of these power structures on the basis of insights from critical international political economy.

The arguments that we present here are likely to provoke quite a high degree of what Pierre Bourdieu (1977) once called "misrecognition." Economists may be perplexed by our premises with regard to economic relationships, as they are based not in neoclassical equilibrium analysis, but rather in the theory of economic dynamics that draws on both an older institutional tradition and neo-Schumpeterian and neo-Marxist economics. We know that our framework troubles European policy analysts whose models, designed for the pragmatic study of "governance," are steeped in the neo-institutional, pluralist, and now constructivist traditions. In contrast to a time—not so many years ago—when there was more openness to these questions (e.g., Lindberg, Alford, Crouch, and Offe, 1975), these scholars may be bemused by our penchant for elite and neo-Marxist theories of the state.

This potential for misrecognition posed a dilemma for us. Clearly, reference needed to be made to literature in these fields in the pursuit of common grounds of understanding and persuasion. At the same time, elaborate literature reviews would have required detours and compromised our goal of advancing our position clearly and succinctly. Our method for dealing with this dilemma was to exercise stringent economy regarding the literature that we comment on and review. Essentially, we followed Gramsci's dictum that, while in warfare one chooses to attack at the weakest point, in intellectual pursuits one attacks at the strongest point.

*   *   *

As is always the case in writing a book, one relies on the collegiality, friendship, and generosity of many people. In that regard, our book does not stray from the norm. In particular, our argument has benefited from constructive criticism at several annual conventions of the International Studies Association, at the Critical Political Economy Research Group of the European Sociological Association, and at The Hague meeting of the Standing Group of International Relations of the European Consortium of Political Research. We have also benefited from presentations we were kindly invited to deliver at the Department of Political Science of the Free University in Amsterdam, the Department of International Relations of the University of Sussex, the European Research Institute of the University of Birmingham, and the Institute for European Studies at Cornell University. Individual colleagues to whom we owe a debt of gratitude include Bastiaan van Apeldoorn, Hans-Jürgen Bieling, Daniele Caramani, Ben Clift, Jan Drahakoupil, Andrew Gamble, Colin Hay, Eric Helleiner, Otto Holman, Laura Horn, Johannes Jäger, Bob Jessop, Paul Lewis, Johnna Montgomery, Nicola Phillips, Kees van der Pijl, Leila Simona Talani, Matthew Watson, and Daniel Wincott. We would like to extend a special thanks to our publisher, Lynne Rienner, whose keen interest and pursuit in maximizing the potential in a book are all too rare. Finally, we think it is high time we recognize and express our thanks to our partners, Mari Assaid and Sushuma Chandrasekhar, who have supported us in so many ways over the years of writing.

Some passages in Chapters, 2, 3, and 4 were published previously in "Monetary Union and the Transatlantic and Social Dimensions of Europe's Crisis," *New Political Economy*, vol. 12, no. 2. They are reprinted here with the permission of Routledge/Taylor and Francis.

1

Introduction:
The Crisis of European Union

SCHOLARSHIP ON THE EUROPEAN UNION has been overtaken by events. During the 1990s the United States outpaced Europe's comparatively sluggish economies and boldly expanded the North Atlantic Treaty Organization (NATO) across the European continent and into the territory of the former Soviet Union. Triumphalists looked forward to a new era of virtually unlimited US power and voiced widespread skepticism concerning the EU's ambitious projects of political and economic union. Yet, the first decade of the twenty-first century has not been kind to the triumphalists. A host of pressing financial problems—not least, the massive and growing current-account deficits—have raised questions about the reserve currency status of a faltering dollar. By exposing the limitations of the vaunted US military machine, the disastrous advance into Iraq and recurrent problems in Afghanistan seem to have shattered the dream of a "new American century."

As US economic and military fortunes declined, observers from all points on the political spectrum and a variety of theoretical perspectives have claimed to discern a tectonic shift in global power relations. Although the specter of Chinese power looms over the horizon, many scholars and journalists have issued enthusiastic proclamations (or dire warnings) of a European challenge to US hegemony (Todd, 2002; Hutton, 2002; Reid, 2004; Kupchan, 2002; Haseler, 2004; Rifkin, 2004; Leonard, 2005; Wallerstein, 2003; McCormick, 2007). The successful launch of the third stage of the Economic and Monetary Union (EMU) in 1999 was widely celebrated as a dramatic forward movement of European regional integration. As the new currency, the euro, soared against a faltering dollar after 2001, much of the skepticism vanished concerning the viability of a monetary union and possibility of preserving a distinctive social model.

1

Symptomatic of this sentiment is the argument of Charles Kupchan, who has proclaimed that "Europe is arriving on the global stage. Now that its single market has been accompanied with a single currency, Europe has a collective weight on matters of trade and finance comparable to that of the United States" (2002: p. 22). In a similar vein, John McCormick has contended that "the EU is a new breed of superpower" within a "postmodern bipolar system" (2007: p. 12). Focusing on the welfare-state policies that for many set Europe's model of capitalism apart from that of the United States, Martin Rhodes and Anton Hemerijck have suggested that the EMU has the capacity to spearhead a successful "self-transformation" of the European social model (Hemerijck, 2002; Rhodes, 2002).

Yet, if economic and political developments of the early twenty-first century have thrown a spotlight on the fragility of US hegemony, they have also confounded predictions of European ascendance and the underlying intellectual assumptions on which these predictions are based. If the bloody occupation of Iraq demonstrated the perils of military over-stretch and hubris for the American superpower, it also exposed deep political divisions that pitted Britain, Italy, Spain, and many new member states of the EU against the Franco-German core and thereby shattered any remaining illusions that Europe could summon the cohesion and political will to serve as a counterweight to the United States.

The successful launch of the euro initially quieted skeptics who had warned that a monetary union bereft of political union was inherently unstable (see, for example, Milward, 1994; Anderson, 1997). Yet, by 2004, a prolonged period of stagnation and mass unemployment compelled first Germany, then France, and finally Italy to breach the walls of the Growth and Stability Pact, thereby exposing the very contradiction of which the skeptics had warned. The so-called reform of 2005 rendered the pact, in the words of the *Financial Times,* "practically worthless" (2005a: p. 12), revealing underlying conflicts of interest among the member states in the eurozone and provoking demands for the renationalization of monetary policy in some quarters amid predictions of impending collapse.[1] Even the soaring euro was a mixed blessing for the EU, as it accelerated the trend toward uneven development and threatened to derail the limited recovery of 2006–2007. The Lisbon Agenda, launched with great fanfare in 2001 to make Europe "the cheapest and easiest place to do business in the world" (European Commission, 2001), has proceeded fitfully in a climate of slow growth and economic nationalism. In 2005, unemployed, trade unionists, youth, and middle-class people uncertain of their economic future in France and the Netherlands decisively repudiated the Constitutional Treaty. Their rebuke to Europe's discredited technocratic elite, what Jean Baudrillard has termed the "complacent coalition around an infallible, universal holy Europe" (2005: p. 24), signified not simply the rejection of an EU treaty, but a broader, systemic crisis of European political representation operating at both the national and supranational levels.

Thus, notwithstanding the United States' own cascading political and economic difficulties, by the middle of 2005 the European project appeared stillborn. Summing up the prevailing sense of malaise, Dominique Moisi (2005: p. 17) outlined three bleak scenarios that contrasted strikingly with the optimism that had accompanied the launch of the euro. Europe might become a "decadent Venice," mired in a "collective acceptance of decay by an entire continent," or a Swiss combination of "selfishness and provincialism." Perhaps even more disconcerting was Moisi's third scenario, "the revenge of nationalism." Former EU commissioners Franz Fischler and Christian Ortner warned that the EU might become "the first empire to go down before it was founded" (Parker and Simonian, 2006: p. 7). Eminent Belgian economist Paul De Grauwe stated flatly that "The monetary union will collapse . . . not next year, but on a time frame of 10 or 20 years" (Kubosova, 2006: p. 1). Europe's leaders proclaimed a period of "reflection" because they could agree on little else. Ironically, the one area on which virtually all Europeans are united is the desire for greater independence from the United States. Yet, growing political fragmentation is making it more difficult to resist the United States' embrace. The multiple and overlapping economic and political crises indicate that the nations of Europe, both collectively and individually, are condemned to experience a long period of turbulence and parochialism. Indeed, even the Schadenfreude with which Washington's congenitally europhobic neoconservatives observe Europe's deepening disarray and inability to mount a coherent challenge to US hegemony is muted by fears that a more fractious European continent will be prone to instability and unable to assist in the United States' imperial project.

This book analyzes the crisis of Europe's second project of integration. The first such project, arising out of Europe's post–World War II economic and geopolitical predicament, sought to prevent another European war through the establishment of limited forms of economic cooperation. While giving rise to the concept of supranational integration, it in fact served to buttress the nation-state and to promote national economic development and political stability (Milward, 1992). The comparatively modest European initiatives were consistent with the main political and economic contours of the social- and Christian-democratic welfare settlements that became institutionalized in the first two decades after World

War II (Milward, 1994). Rhetoric aside, the EU was not during this phase an important independent factor in European or international affairs. The antidemocratic features of the EU were consequently of little import when, with the partial exceptions of agriculture and trade, economic policies were largely under the control of the member states.

Europe's second integrationist project resulted from François Mitterrand's decisive U-turn from national Keynesianism to market integration in the early 1980s and was effectively launched by the 1983 realignment of the European Monetary System (EMS) and the Fontainebleau Summit of 1984. The key institutional expressions of this project are the Single European Act (SEA) of 1987, the Treaty on European Union of 1993 (the Maastricht Treaty), and, more recently, the European Constitutional Treaty, which was signed in 2004 but faltered in the ratification process because of the referenda results in France and the Netherlands. Although greatly assisted by the new domestic and international political landscape resulting from German reunification and the end of the Cold War, the second project is based on the assumption uniting parties of the center-right and center-left that a decade of stagflation and failed attempts at European monetary coordination after the collapse of the Bretton Woods system mean that there is "no alternative" to national and regional neoliberalism. Spelling out the full implications of this assumption, the Constitutional Treaty—a quintessentially neoliberal and Atlanticist document—abandons distinctive commitments to social solidarity and social rights that are inherent in national constitutions or previous EU treaties. Unlike normal constitutions, which define institutions and enshrine fundamental rights, it elucidates the principle of "a highly competitive market economy" (TCE, Article I-3(2), 2004) with extraordinary clarity.[2]

Notwithstanding its underlying neoliberal logic, the second integrationist project has been marketed in European mass politics in a much more equivocal way. Indeed, more often than not it has been presented as a defense of the "European social model" (Hufbauer, 2006). Whether this approach to marketing and presentation reflects sincere conviction or instrumental political calculation, it reveals the tension between the "permissive consensus" of the economic policy concept of elites and the imperatives of mass politics in European civil societies deriving from distinctive commitments to social solidarity and full employment.

If the first integrationist project reinforced the power of the nation-state by facilitating the social- and Christian-democratic welfare settlements, the implications of Europe's neoliberal relaunching for the nation-state are more ambiguous, and potentially perilous. The single market and, even more dramatically, the monetary union have greatly reduced national prerogatives without giving rise to the pan-European democratic polity necessary to lend stability and cohesion to these radical developments. This project was brought into disarray in 2004 by the collapse of the Growth and Stability Pact (GSP) as it was originally conceived, an agreement that was intended to resolve this contradiction. Perhaps even more notable was the challenge issued by substantial popular mobilization in the Netherlands and France against a Constitutional Treaty that enshrined neoliberalism and Atlanticism.

The crisis to which we refer in this book is thus not simply that of Europe's Economic and Monetary Union, but rather more broadly the exhaustion of a two-decade-long phase of neoliberal economic integration that has condemned Europe to slow growth and mass unemployment, has weakened traditional forms of political and social solidarity at the national and regional levels, and has further subordinated the EU to an increasingly violent and unsteady US imperium. Our analysis runs contrary to the idealized, teleological narrative that has been a recurrent feature of mainstream scholarship and journalism on the European Union for two generations. Supranational institutions and ideas have not in themselves been the most important factors in European integration. Rather, they have played a decisive role only to the extent that they have successfully articulated the interests and strategies of the dominant national, regional, and transatlantic social forces. We argue that the contemporary predicament of the EU does not arise naturally from a crisis of *integration per se,* or the growing pains that might inevitably be expected to arise as the union enlarges and governance is gradually shifted from the national state to supranational institutions. To be sure, nationalism, institutional paralysis, and failures of leadership—the usual suspects—persist and, indeed, have become more pronounced. However, we understand Europe's contemporary predicament in terms of the internal contradictions and limitations of neoliberalism and the concomitant subordination to the United States. Such an analysis provides a deeper and more comprehensive understanding of contemporary European society and politics.[3]

It is perhaps also important to indicate what we are *not* arguing. First, emphasizing neoliberal underpinnings of the second integration project while criticizing idealism is not a contradiction. We do *not* think that one has said everything that is important about actors when one has labeled them "neoliberal." Rather, in our view social forces, state managers, supranational entrepreneurs, and other actors embrace, tactically adjust themselves toward, or resist neoliberalism from the vantage points of different, and often competing, material positions and interests.

Above all, we do not suggest that the neoliberal European project is a conspiracy—a fully thought out blueprint immanently implemented, and globally mastered, by its agents. We rather subscribe to a more structural point of view, in which neoliberalism describes an "institutional materiality"—a set of intersubjective norms and rules to which actors have to orient themselves (Poulantzas, 1973: p. 115)—or, for that matter, a "logic of appropriateness" (March and Olsen, 1989: p. 161). These norms and rules, in turn, reflect a structural matrix of institutions that define the formal separation of politics and economics in the prevailing regulatory mode of capitalist development. Especially important in this context has been the organization of finance, which systematically favors the United States. It is in this sense that the United States remains hegemonic, albeit not without a growing list of challengers. This is a position that we amplify in Chapter 2.

Our *analytical focus* on EMU reflects the centrality of money and finance in transatlantic and European regional power relations. In a classic formulation, David Calleo has highlighted the importance of money for social and political relations in general: "International economic relations are highly politicized. This is particularly true of monetary relations, the history of which often serves as a metaphor for general political-economic relations in the world system" (Calleo, 2003: p. 1). Similarly, drawing on Georg Simmel and Niklas Luhmann, Claus Offe (1985) has emphasized the importance of money and finance as central "steering media" through which capitalist states perform their contradictory roles of rendering compatible economic dynamism, social legitimation, and internal operational cohesion (see also Jessop, 1990: pp. 307–337). The EMU, then, can be seen as constituting the institutional fulcrum of the neoliberal integrationist project. Nevertheless, the *scope* of this book goes well beyond the question of money and monetary union. From our chosen analytical vantage point, we offer a holistic analysis of the interconnections of socioeconomic dynamics, the welfare state, questions of legitimacy and citizenship, and Europe's geopolitical predicament.

Hegemony cannot be reduced to "institutional copying." To assert that the EU is pursuing a neoliberal project does not imply that either the EU itself or its individual nation-states can entirely abandon distinctive institutions or values that have been shaped by centuries of historical experience. Europe will never become "Americanized" or even "Anglicized" in this sense. Rather, hegemony means that norms and rules successfully represent certain particular interests as general interests. Hence, the fact that the EMU is institutionally different from the

Federal Reserve System is not an indicator of the absence of hegemony, especially not the fact that the European Central Bank (ECB) has to be more neoliberal than the Fed.[4] This is an argument we amplify also in Chapter 2.

This emphasis on structure does not imply that structures can exist outside the beliefs and practices of agents or that the strategies of agents are not important. Rather, it assumes that agents are always situated in structural relationships that give them a partial view of the terrain on which they operate and partial capacities to shape institutions and structures. Nevertheless, the capacities of some are more partial than others. Bob Jessop's (1990: p. 359) characterization of "strategic coordination" comes close to our understanding of agency:

> Since the structure of the social world is always more complex than any social force can conceive and its overall evolution lies beyond the control of any social force, strategic coordination can only occur in the context of uncontrolled and anarchic structural coupling of co-evolving structures. But this does not mean that it is impossible to intervene in this evolutionary process and produce results.

The US state strategy we describe in Chapter 2 as a "hegemonic strategy" can indeed be seen as an example of such intervention "producing results."

Finally, neoliberalism in Europe is neither homogenous over countries, regions, and sectors nor a fully realized outcome. Indeed, in many respects it is precisely the incompleteness of neoliberalism and its differential and uneven effects on classes, states, and regions that exacerbate Europe's crisis. From the organization of the single market through the EMU, neoliberal forces are connected with and reorganize other instituted socioeconomic practices, such as collective bargaining regimes and welfare-state settlements. Neoliberal forces do not always eliminate these regimes and settlements, although the latter must be reconstituted to become compatible with the neoliberal framework. In addition, as we show in Chapter 3, in certain locales at certain times EMU-induced neoliberalism is even rendered compatible with a reinvigoration of export-oriented welfare settlements that have significant mercantilist dimensions. However, the result of these settlements is chronic division within Europe, which prevents the forging of a common strategy of action to address economic stagnation, the political crisis of representation, and subordination to the United States.

This book is organized into six chapters. In Chapter 2, we present a set of key concepts and a historically informed account for understanding

Europe's continuing subordination to US-dominated global finance. Our central concept is *minimal hegemony:* The development of the international political economy (IPE) as a discipline in the late 1960s coincided with an impending transformation of global economic and political power. In seeking to understand the nature of this transformation, conventional scholarship relied on "basic force" models of international power relations, which derive power more or less straightforwardly from the possession of resources (Gilpin, 1973; Keohane, 1980). Yet, basic force models of power fail to take into account the structural aspects of power, especially the power rooted in the United States' domination of global finance. Accounts of a gathering European economic challenge to the United States overlook the deeper and more salient structural features of the Euro-Atlantic relationship as it has developed since the fall of the Bretton Woods system in the early 1970s.

A structural account of power, by contrast, draws attention to the dynamics of the social, political, and economic terrain (Cox, 1987; Strange, 1986; Cafruny, 1990; Gill and Law, 1989). Prevailing structures constrain the actions of some actors while enabling others. Basic force models, grounded in productivity and national output, made some sense prior to 1971, when US financial and monetary policies were constrained by the linkage of the dollar to gold, however tenuous this became throughout the 1960s. By the 1980s, US elites had developed a new strategy of hegemonic coordination to resolve the post–Bretton Woods crisis. We distinguish this *minimal hegemonic* strategy from the *integral hegemony* that prevailed during the heyday of the Bretton Woods system. During the *integral* phase, the United States was prepared to make material concessions to its European allies and to sponsor massive material support (such as Marshall Plan aid) to promote systemic stability and legitimacy. By contrast, in the contemporary phase of *minimal hegemony,* the United States draws on its structural power to pursue a more narrowly based policy that externalizes domestic social and political problems. The system nevertheless remains hegemonic in a minimal sense, since structures and intersubjective norms compel subordinate social forces to consent to the prevailing order.

Hence, the progressive deregulation of financial markets that unfolded during the 1980s and the 1990s has served to reconfigure the international political economy to enable the United States to reproduce its hegemony despite its relative industrial decline. The European social model was facilitated by and dependent upon the permissive structures of the dollar-gold system under US tutelage during the phase of *integral hegemony.* Yet, Europe's subordination to the new finance-based structural configuration has progressively undercut the economic and political foundations of this model.

We should emphasize that this is not an impact study that draws comparisons between the EMU and the EMS. Of course, in many crucial respects the EMU represents a radical departure from all previous attempts at monetary coordination, including the EMS; in other respects, however, it is possible to identify important continuities. Both are institutional expressions of a regional monetary order that is embedded in the post–Bretton Woods transnational financial market structure and that orders power relations between the United States and European political economies. It is also important to reiterate, in this context, the distinction between *structural power,* where the social terrain is systematically ordered in favor of some over others regardless of action, and *relational power,* where the possessor of power has to act in order to make a subordinate "do what s/he otherwise would not do" (Lukes, 1974). Of course, the EMU is not a US creation. Indeed, many of its proponents view it as a means of counterbalancing US power. From time to time, moreover, US government officials, think tanks, and financial institutions have expressed concerns about the potential long-term threat to US interests posed by EMU. However, the transnational financial architecture in which the EMU is embedded, to no little extent shaped by the leadership of US policymakers and business, is ultimately a reflection of the United States' structural power.

We explore the socioeconomic implications of Europe's subordination with respect to this structural power in Chapter 3. The US Federal Reserve presides over a system that is inherently expansionary as a result of the special role of US financial markets. By contrast, reflecting the different position the European economy occupies in the circuits of global capital, EMU firmly subordinates macroeconomic policy to short-term global financial markets in such a way that the expansion of liquidity becomes conditioned on the disciplinary judgments those markets make on the performance of European export sectors, relieved only by bouts of mercantilist depreciation. This approach initially arose out of the imperatives of the niche strategy of the West German "model," which was generalized and internalized to the other member states through the Exchange Rate Mechanism (ERM) and the terms of the European Monetary Cooperation Fund. Under EMU, European macroeconomics continues to function in a similar way, facilitating competition between individual niche strategies rather than strategically coordinating an embryonic European macroeconomy. This is the effect, inter alia, of the asymmetry between a supranational monetary policy, an essentially intergovernmentalist fiscal policy, and a tenuous Growth and Stability Pact, the minimalist "negative integration" of mutual recognition that characterizes the single market, the deregulation of financial services, and the attendant disorganization of Europe's national systems of corporate governance. The "open method of coordination" in labor market and industrial policy complements this pattern.

Given the constraints operating on the ECB, flexible labor markets—or structural reforms—are offered as the cure for eurosclerosis and, indeed, as the only means of preserving monetary union. Hence, the EU has sought to replicate the Anglo-US model of labor flexibility and deregulation, while rejecting its emphasis on macroeconomic promotion of growth. Yet, flexible labor markets and capital mobility exacerbate, rather than resolve, the problem of low growth and high unemployment. The ensemble of competing niche strategies in a single space of economic competition is self-limiting because it generates a "game" of competitive austerity (Albo, 1994) among the constituent parts. In this game, each unit reduces domestic demand as part of its export-oriented production strategy wherein wage increases and benefits are kept below productivity growth rates. This reduces consumption and concentrates productivity gains on corporations, the value of which is stored and transacted in financial networks. To be sure, the game results in "winning" states and regions, but the overall effect has been economic stagnation. Effective demand expansion has been inadequate throughout the eurozone. This, in turn, has had detrimental effects on output and productivity, due to the lack of adequate investment levels and a stable environment in which to transfer the potentials of new technology into practical economic innovation so essential for the institutional framework of "social market economies" (Boyer, 2000).

European elites have argued that the neoliberal integration politics of the post-Maastricht era are compatible with the social- and Christian-democratic variants of the European social model. Yet, the economic stagnation that follows the pursuit of "competitive austerity" places ever-greater pressure on the social model and requires political elites continuously to seek to renegotiate societal accords in response to the alleged necessities of the global market and to demographic pressures in a postindustrial society. In other words, Europe's subordinate participation within the transatlantic order, as structured by finance, preempts the possibility of resolving structural problems associated with postindustrial—or, as we prefer, post-Fordist—transformation in a way that is compatible with social- and Christian-democratic accords. As Chapter 4 shows, the result at the national level has been an organic crisis of the European social model, in which traditional distinctions between right and left have been rendered virtually meaningless and reform is understood primarily in terms of market rationality. Notwithstanding obligatory appeals to social solidarity, welfare-state retrenchment and labor-market flexibility have become the stated practical goal of all parties. Implementation of these policies follows a logic that is determined by the ebb and flow of grassroots militancy and protest voting, and not party political mobilization or the nominal ideology of the governing party. As traditional social and Christian democracy unravels, the national political arena acquires a postmodern character. Political parties are being transformed into electoral machines and decoupled from family, church, unions, and other social movements. This renders them slavishly dependent on an increasingly commercialized mass media. Populism and far-right parties and movements flourish in this environment.

At the EU level, popular mobilizations—largely independent of existing party structures—have directly focused on the contradiction between neoliberal norms and the desire to maintain the social model. The referenda of 2005 in the Netherlands and France, in which popular sentiment could not be mediated by political parties, illustrate the difficulties of postmodern neoliberalism as a viable articulating principle for further European integration. Yet, no convincing alternative has yet emerged.

In the wake of the constitutional failure, policymakers have slowly started to search for pragmatic consensus toward future EU policies. While a modest vision of incrementalism has obvious appeal,[5] it does not fully comprehend the political and economic implications of Europe's second project and thus underestimates the depth of the contemporary crisis. The formation of the eurozone and the attendant liberalization of an enlarged Union represent radical and destabilizing developments. The failure to construct a corresponding polity portends growing social and economic instability and political fragmentation.

Chapter 5 returns to the transatlantic relationship and considers the implications for Europe of growing challenges to US hegemony in the form of massive budget and trade deficits and the unraveling of the neoconservative project in Iraq and the wider Middle East. Because market integration has been accompanied not by political centralization but rather by fragmentation and "variable geometry," the EU has become a sprawling, multitiered entity comprising a eurozone minus the UK—a free-trading zone absent a common fiscal and tax policy, with new

member states whose second- and even third-class status and geopolitical vulnerability drive them into the arms of Washington and NATO.
Following a brief period of uncertainty in the early 1990s, the United
States gradually expanded its geopolitical reach into Central and Eastern Europe through interventions in the Balkans, the enlargement of
NATO, and the establishment of close links to Atlanticist and neoliberal
factions in the new member states. The corollary of "flower revolutions" has been a transformation of the United States' military posture
as new bases have been established or are projected in Kosovo, Poland,
the Czech Republic, Romania, Bulgaria, and Central Asia. The fiscal
and monetary constraints of EMU have foreclosed the possibility that
the core European powers could expand significantly their own military
establishments and provide an alternative to the hub-and-spoke system
that Washington has constructed.

Notwithstanding the growth of US economic and military power in
Europe and Central Asia, many questions remain concerning the future
trajectory of US hegemony. Does neoconservative leadership of a faltering advance into Iraq and, perhaps, Iran reflect an objective national interest in world power and control of global energy resources and transit
routes, or does it reflect ideological factors and the irrationalities and particularities of US domestic politics? Will the failure to stabilize Iraq have
long-term consequences for US power in the Middle East and beyond?
How long can foreign central banks and investors continue to finance the
current US account deficit and maintain the value of the dollar?

A "terminal crisis" of US hegemony (Arrighi, 2005b: p. 83; see also
Wallerstein, 2003; Golub, 2004) would establish the structural conditions for a putative "European challenge." Yet, Chapter 6 concludes on
a more cautious note. To be sure, no global hierarchy lasts forever. The
dangers and uncertainties resulting from the geopolitical miscalcula-
tions and blunders of the Bush administration render hazardous any predictions concerning the future course of US hegemony. Still, expectations of hegemonic decline, now in play for more than a generation, may
be premature. Notwithstanding the dollar's weaknesses, no other currency appears capable of taking its place for the foreseeable future. Nor
does a single state or group of states appear likely in the next decade to
have the capability to challenge the United States' preeminent geopolitical position. In this context, the inability to generate a stable growth
trajectory from within means that Europe's fortunes remain hostage to
the US "growth locomotive" and to monetary and fiscal policies that
reflect US priorities. Absent the fundamental social and political changes
that might engender a positive and coherent regional agency, Europe

appears condemned to continuing dependency on the United States' precarious imperium.

Notes

1. Roberto Maroni, Italy's welfare minister, called in June 2005 for Italy to return to the lira. Prime Minister Silvio Berlusconi complained that "Prodi's euro conned us all." Tony Barber, "Italian Premier Rounds on the Euro," *Financial Times,* July 29, 2005, p. 2. See also Wolfgang Munchau, "Is the Euro Forever? As the Strains Turn to Pain, Its Foundations Look Far from Secure," *Financial Times,* June 8, 2005, p. 15; Daniel Gros, Thomas Mayer, and Angel Ubide, *Euro at Risk,* Seventh Annual Report of the Centre for European Policy Studies Macroeconomic Policy Group, Brussels (June 2005); David Hale, "Could Italy Be First to Leave the Euro?" *European Affairs* (Summer 2005). See also Paul De Grauwe (2006a, p. 1).

2. For example, Article III redefines "public services" as "services of general economic interest." Article III-166-2 stipulates that "undertakings entrusted with the operation of services of general economic interest or having the character of an income-producing monopoly shall be subject to the provisions of the constitution, in particular to the rules on competition." Article III-167-1 bans "any aid granted by a member state or through state resources in any form whatsoever which distorts or threatens to distort competition." Whereas national constitutions (e.g., the French and Italian ones) establish a "right to work," the treaty recognizes "the right to engage in work" (III-75-1) and "the freedom to seek employment, to work, to exercise the right of establishment and to provide services in any member state" (II-75-2). Notwithstanding its ambiguities, a review of the text in its totality makes it hard to avoid the conclusion that the Constitutional Treaty is a quintessentially neoliberal document. In 2,002 pages of main text, the word "bank" or its derivative appears 176 times, followed by "market" (88); "trade" (38); "competition" (29); "capital" (23); and "commodity" (11). Cassen (2005, p. 1).

3. A comprehensive critique of the theoretical literature on the EU can be found in our recent anthology, *A Ruined Fortress? Neoliberal Hegemony and Transformation in Europe* (Cafruny and Ryner, 2003); see especially chapter 1 of that anthology.

4. This is not to say that a degree of institutional copying is not taking place. As Lenka Polackova's Ph.D. thesis (2004) has shown, financial reform in Europe, in the direction of a more "Anglo-Saxon model," has often been devised within the procedures of the Basel Agreements by national central bankers. This has set the agenda for EU financial-market reform, where EU jurisprudence and the legislative power of the Commission are mobilized.

5. For example, Andrew Moravcsik asserts that "EU institutions actually function rather well. To judge by results rather than rhetoric, the last decade ranks as one of the EU's best: enlargement, the Euro, and increasingly coherent internal and external policies" (2006a: p. B2).

2

Transatlantic Dimensions

While we like to believe that purely economic competition, properly conducted, leads to mutual economic gain, we cannot deny that transatlantic relationships are highly politicised. This is particularly true of monetary relations, the history of which often serves as a metaphor for the underlying geopolitical balance between Europe and America.

—David Calleo (2003: p. 1)

The predictions of a "European challenge" that accompanied the launch of the euro expressed the hopes and dreams of many people in the United States and Europe, but they were based on incorrect and misleading assumptions about the nature and scope of US hegemonic power in relation to Europe. A structural conception of power, emphasizing the centrality of US financial leadership in the broader context of geopolitical supremacy, leads to a very different conclusion: the aspiration of the European elite to build a monetary union to promote competitiveness, regional autonomy, and sustained growth is self-limiting. This is because the project of monetary union as it has developed since the Maastricht Treaty is inherently connected to a US-led, neoliberal, transnational financial and monetary order that displaces economic and social contradictions from the United States to other parts of the world, including Europe.

We begin this chapter with a preliminary theoretical discussion. This is necessary in order to clarify the meaning of some of the central terms and concepts that we use, including *crisis, US hegemony,* and *nature of the contemporary nation-state.* We then propose the ideal types of *integral* and *minimal hegemony* and show how each of these forms of power is associated with a particular set of national and international political and social dynamics. In the second part of this chapter, we use these concepts to describe the transformation of Euro-US political and economic relations that resulted from the collapse of the Bretton Woods system and the advent of neoliberalism. This sets the stage for the third part, where we account for Europe's contemporary impasse.

Theoretical Considerations: Crisis, Hegemony, and the Nation-State

The use of the term *crisis* is of course commonplace. It is more often than not vaguely deployed, and sometimes incautiously so, especially on the left. The failure of the Constitutional Treaty in 2005 abruptly triggered widespread lamentations of a "European crisis" from scholars, journalists, and politicians in national capitals as well as in Brussels (e.g., Jervis, 2005). To be sure, the failure of the Constitutional Treaty provides abundant evidence of such a crisis. However, our use of the term is more comprehensive and certainly more provocative than the use of it in most of these accounts. Europe's crisis, we argue, does not arise primarily from flawed or obsolescent institutional design, insufficient leadership, or lack of communication. The *nons* and *nees* ("nays") of the referenda are one expression among many of a deeper crisis of social and political legitimacy that has resulted from the structural consequences of Europe's acquiescence to what we call "minimal US hegemony." Neoliberal Europe is eroding its distinctive social models and traditional mass parties without an adequate preparation of the social and political terrain. The result is an uncertain and potentially ominous future.

Crisis

Jürgen Habermas (1975: pp. 1–4) proposed an eminently useful definition of the concept of *crisis,* understood from this more comprehensive vantage point. Social scientists have inherited the term from two distinct sources that together capture two important sides of the same coin. From medicine, we understand crisis as "the phase of an illness in which it is decided whether the organism's self-healing powers are sufficient for recovery" (p. 1). This definition invites us to address the concerns of structural functionalism with the "permissible limits" of reproduction of a social system (e.g., Runciman, 1963: p. 114). While there are good reasons to be wary of the biological metaphor of social relations that this approach implies, the functionalist approach has the distinct advantage of directing attention to the crucial questions of how highly differentiated social orders might work and, as permissible limits are violated, disintegrate. This limited subscription to functionalism is different from the functionalist fallacy, where one assumes that something must happen because the system "requires" it to happen. On the basis of this understanding of crisis, we argue that the European social system, or systems, that the EMU is supposed to help regulate are unlikely to be maintained within "permissible limits," given the national and regional pressures arising as a result of the EMU's design. In short, we argue that the EMU imposes a macroeconomic stance on the European economy that prevents the latter from achieving and generalizing a level of output and productivity growth required to maintain welfare-state provisions and entitlements compatible with prevailing norms of social citizenship. This, in turn, exacerbates political conflicts within and between member states and hampers the development of an effective political agency.

Classical aesthetics, such as dramatic tragedy, supplies a second— but related—meaning of *crisis,* which, in contrast to the previous definition, invokes agency and its identity. Here, crises are turning points in a fateful process:

> Fate is fulfilled in the revelation of conflicting norms against which the identities of the participants shatter, unless they are able to summon up the strength to win back their freedom by shattering the mythical power of fate through the formation of new identities. (Habermas, 1975: p. 2)

These two conceptions of crisis can be synthesized as a refinement of Antonio Gramsci's understanding of an "organic crisis" in which there is a profound contradiction between "structures and superstructures" and "where the old is dying, but the new is yet to be born" (1971: pp. 175–185, 210–218, 365–366). We argue that it is becoming increasingly difficult, within a framework of neoliberal economic governance, to maintain a harmonious equation between the norms of transatlantic partnership under US leadership and the entrenched (for the most part, Christian-democratic) social citizenship norms of European welfare capitalism. Grave doubts are also justified concerning Europeans' capacity to find a way out of the resulting impasse: to "summon adequate strength" either to shatter the mythical powers of these norms, or to abandon them.

Hegemony and the Nation-State

The second concept that is central to our argument is *US hegemony,* which implies assigning a continued central importance of the nation-state in the global political economy. Questions concerning the contemporary nature, status, capacities, and indeed relevance of the nation-state are central to the globalization debate (for polar-opposite views, see, for example, Ohmae, 1990, and Hirst and Thompson, 1996). Whatever else can be said about this debate, certainly the neorealist axiomatic postulate that the nation-state is the only relevant subject and object of hegemony has been put in severe doubt. Whether this warrants the claim that we now live in a "post-Westphalian" era (Cox, 1992; Cameron and Palan, 1999; Caporaso, 2000) is less certain.

Concepts such as "European system" (Hix, 1999), "multilevel governance" (Hooghe and Marks, 2001), and, indeed, "transnational capitalist class" (van Apeldoorn, 2002), reflecting a variety of theoretical perspectives, have cast doubt on the central importance of the state in the European political economy. Because certain juridical and managerial functions required to facilitate the operation of capitalist economies have clearly been internationalized (Cutler, 2003), each of these concepts offers considerable heuristic value in drawing attention to significant limitations to, or at least complications of, sovereignty. This is not the least the case in Europe, given the status that the principle of "direct effect" assigns to EU law. Also, overarching "comprehensive concepts of control," giving cohesion and direction to transnational capitalism, are important (van der Pijl, 1984; 1998; van Apeldoorn, 2002; see also Gill, 1990).

We believe, however, that abandoning the nation-state prefix to hegemony is premature. The juridical and managerial functions in question—and comprehensive concepts of control—do depend, in the last instance, on the authority required to collectively bind decisions in a given territory. This authority—known as sovereignty—still resides with nation-states. In that regard, the latter remain crucial as authors of international agreements and treaties (Panitch, 1994). But there are even further crucial factors that ensure the continued salience of the nation-state. It is above all the nation-state that maintains societal legitimacy by mediating the tendentially antagonistic relations *between* classes. Particularly important is the way in which electoral systems, involving national particularities of political cleavages, and welfare-state arrangements, which crucially include the power of taxation, distance political rule overtly from the class structure (Panitch and Gindin, 2005: pp. 102–104; see also Bendix, 1977; Therborn, 1980). To this we should add the reproductive functions of the welfare state, essential since the inception of industrial capitalism (Wilensky, 1975; Therborn, 1987). There is no obvious substitute for the nation-state in the performance of these functions, which are essential for social stability. Transnational agreements over comprehensive socioeconomic concepts of control have not eliminated national power blocs or the struggles among them; they express a particular balance of power among them, not their negation.

The foregoing underlines the complex character of the state in modern and highly differentiated social formations. The state is not a "thing," but an ensemble of social relations between different branches, with different specializations, terms of reference, and functions (Allison, 1972; Poulantzas, 1978; Lindblom, 1980). It is with reference to this complexity that we can understand the manner in which the EU and its member states actively and entirely at their own volition constructed a monetary union that was consistent with their own subordination to the United States. Particularly important has been the pivotal role of central bankers in designing the EMU and the terms of contestability over its design, in the context of a US-centered, transnational financial structure (Verdun, 1999). Notably, central bankers serve almost exclusively economic management—not societal legitimation—functions. As such, in effect, they have served the interests of transatlantic-European economic-corporate interests, which are deeply entwined with US capitalism (Panitch and Gindin, 2005: pp. 106–113, 115–118),[1] and which have adjusted their strategies to US-led transatlanticism.[2] This has produced a set of profound difficulties for the state apparatuses and party systems charged with mediating economic imperatives with societal legitimacy. EMU design has also been consistent with the export-niche strategies of some smaller states and regions and their internal social settlements. In the era of the EMS, this was also the case with the West German state, which was crucial in lending central bankers adequate authority to shape the EMU (Verdun, 1999). But this has been at the expense of both the long-term growth prospects of the European economy as a whole and the capacities of other state apparatuses, whose role it is to balance capital accumulation and societal legitimation imperatives in Europe. Hence, one should not conclude that "what is good for DaimlerChrysler" is necessarily "good for Europe." Also, the fact that structural conditions no longer obtain for a continuation of Germany's niche strategy serves as a profound source of European instability. We will return to these issues in Chapters 3 and 4.

Integral Hegemony and Minimal Hegemony

For Gramsci, power had many forms and variants, ranging from the purely coercive and visible to the consensual and invisible. A ruling group is hegemonic because it is capable of universalizing its interests, albeit not without contradictions:

> The fact of hegemony presupposes that account be taken of the interests and tendencies of the groups over which hegemony is to be exercised, and that a certain compromise equilibrium should be formed— in other words, that the leading group should make sacrifices of an economic-corporate kind. (1971: p. 161)

Integral hegemony refers to the strongest and most consolidated form of power (Cafruny, 1990). It describes highly stable relations characterized by a well-developed sense of common purpose and lack of overt antagonism among various groups. The hegemonic power is capable simultaneously of satisfying its own economic interests and those of the system as a whole. The concept of integral hegemony is useful in describing the Bretton Woods system in its formative years, an "embedded liberal" order (Ruggie, 1982) based on a high level of consensus within the Euro-Atlantic area and significant concessions by the United States. By contrast, *minimal hegemony* describes an international system in which important contradictions have developed between the interests of the ruling and subordinate groups. The hegemon is no longer strong enough to systematically devise policies capable of serving general interests. The system is unstable, but coercion is minimized because subordinate groups and, crucially, the elites who might potentially represent them, are too weak and disorganized to consolidate a counter-hegemonic bloc, especially since the immediate material interests of some within the potentially rival elite may be served by the prevailing order. Potential opposition is decapitated and impotent. A continued prevalence of consent gives this order a hegemonic quality, and it is not merely based on domination. What is lacking is the ability of either the ruling group or the opposition to resolve systemic contradictions, resulting in a process of drift and chronic instability.

Minimal hegemony, we contend, provides a more accurate depiction of the dynamics of relations *between* Europe and the United States as they have unfolded since the collapse of the Bretton Woods order, than "domination without hegemony" (Guha, 1992; Arrighi, 2005a). Nevertheless, we argue that it is a central dimension of the organic crisis *within* Europe that the US state is using its minimal hegemonic status to displace and externalize social contradictions into the international system, which in turn are, in part, internalized in Europe. Minimal hegemony implies that there is a substantial transatlantic accord among elites, albeit an unequal one. Neoliberal ideology, which has defined the content of Euro-US relations since the collapse of the Bretton Woods system, still cements capitalist ruling classes and elites together in an organic alliance. From within the terms of this intersubjective agreement, the United States continues to provide "collective goods" in the form of liquidity, trade liberalization, and security, although very much on its own terms. Although institutional arrangements increasingly fail to provide material concessions consistent with civil societal norms of Europe's social accords, there is not a sufficiently strong countermovement to challenge this order on the ethicopolitical level. Yet, the cumulative effect can be, as in the case of contemporary Europe, an emergent crisis.

Global Finance and Changes in US Hegemony Since the Collapse of Bretton Woods

The post–World War II order rested on two pillars. The first was Fordist regulation, which emerged in the United States in the 1930s and became generalized throughout the OECD (Organization of Economic Cooperation and Development) area in the post–World War II era. Fordism, with liberal, social-democratic, and Christian-democratic variations, depended on the linkage of mass production and consumption through Keynesianism. Technological innovation and collective agreements made possible welfare expansion and the distribution of productivity gains. The second pillar was US hegemony, expressed in interdependent monetary and trade policies. Through the dollar-gold standard, the United States provided stability and liquidity, laying the basis for the expansion of trade and investment, which, however, lagged behind the growth of output. Keynesian mutual recognition of capital controls was designed to thwart "unproductive" financial flows (Helleiner, 1994: pp. 25–50). This regime made it possible to balance the management of the international economy with sufficient state autonomy to mediate distinct welfare arrangements (Ruggie, 1982: pp. 195–232). The system remained stable as long as the dollar was strong enough to generate a constant supply of liquidity and international capital flows remained low in proportion to GDP.

Monetarism and US Predatory Policies

By the late 1960s, the twin pillars of this integral hegemony were crumbling. As the United States' perceived capacity to redeem dollar holdings with gold at the value fixed by Bretton Woods diminished, confidence in the dollar waned, and Europe and Japan became increasingly reluctant to finance US deficits (Block, 1977; Parboni, 1982). At the same time, Fordism began to experience strains as two decades of full employment eroded wage restraint, especially in the context of inflationary US policies; the productive system was running into its limits of expansion as price competition from east Asia intensified in Fordist core sectors and the rate of profit fell (Glyn, Lipietz, Hughes, and Singh, 1990; Brenner, 2006).[3] Socioeconomically, the strain reflected competing interests and conceptions in attempts to respond to Fordist crisis (Lipietz, 1985).

The initial response on both sides of the Atlantic was to seek to preserve the framework of embedded liberalism through a revision of the terms of agreement between the United States and Europe. The unilateral US decision to decouple the dollar from gold in 1971 did not, however, portend the decline of hegemony and the emergence of a multilateral balance of power, as assumed by numerous US scholars. Rather, it ushered in the phase of considerably more unstable minimal hegemony involving the more predatory use of power by the United States. Policies began to reflect more narrowly defined national objectives and interests, and a narrower social base (Calleo, 1982). Thus, during the 1970s, US foreign economic policy became more immediately self-interested; expansionary fiscal and monetary policies transmitted inflation to Western Europe, igniting oil price increases and undermining Europe's attempts to maintain stable exchange rates.

By 1980, however, US inflation was in double digits, and speculation against the dollar began to mount, triggering the "Volcker shock" as the US Federal Reserve adopted a highly monetarist stance, which caused a worldwide increase of interest rates and resulted in progressively increasing financial inflows to the United States. Under the Reagan presidency, interest rates were kept high, as was the value of the dollar. Tax cuts and massive increases in military expenditure meant that the tight monetary policy was accompanied with a lax fiscal policy. During this period, the United States "learned" that it had the structural capacity to live with chronic fiscal and balance-of-payments deficits and, moreover, that these deficits could be used to limit government spending on social programs. The rest of the world, of course, paid dearly for this policy stance. The high interest rates set off the Third World debt crisis and cast much of the world into depression as commodity prices tumbled.

High interest rates also added to the stagflation woes of most European countries, which, in contrast to the United States, did not have the structural means to pursue domestically induced reflation.

Thus, the increasing autonomy that derived from decoupling the dollar from gold allowed the United States to carry out with greater impunity fiscal and monetary policies that reflected domestic preoccupations and interests. In the Carter phase of the Fordist crisis, the decline of the dollar and resulting global inflation impeded Europe's attempts to recover from the recession by increasing exports and eventually provoked a European response in the form of a Franco-German bid for a zone of European monetary stability. But this initiative collapsed in 1979 as European currencies appreciated at different rates and attempts to coordinate policy failed. During the Reagan/Volcker phase, matters worked differently. The appreciation of the dollar provided the basis for export-oriented recovery in a monetarist setting, especially for Germany and other European countries specializing in high value–added manufactured goods, but also for some other, smaller corporatist states (Lankowski, 1982; Ryner, 2003; Katzenstein, 1985). Henceforth, monetarism came to enjoy a wide ideological appeal, as it was seen as anchoring incomes policies. Other European countries, such as France, saw no alternative but to attempt to copy this strategy, although here accommodation was more tactical; all-out conversion to monetarist ideology was also less widespread among elites (Clift, 2003: pp. 178–183).

Nevertheless, what Stephen Gill (1998: pp. 157–196) has called neo-constitutional "disciplinary neo-liberalism" was generalized in Europe through, inter alia, regionally fixed exchange rates tied to the German mark and short-term transnational financial movements. This refers to a governance practice of binding discrete, day-to-day policy through framework agreements in order to insulate policymakers from demands of social groups for protection against the market. This practice is also intended to socialize such groups and actors to behave in a market-conforming manner. This provided the backdrop for the more successful relaunch of the EMS and the ERM in 1983. Through the EMS, monetarism and price stability were generalized in Europe, but at a high cost in terms of unemployment. In this phase, consolidated by the Louvre and Plaza agreements, formal transatlantic cooperation was established on this new foundation.

US Structural Power

To understand the dynamics noted above, it is important to specify the nature of US structural power that had accumulated by the time of the collapse of the Bretton Woods system, and when the decision was made to let the dollar float. The primary rationale offered for floating exchange rates was that this would relieve countries from having to pursue domestic austerity in order to fulfil international obligations. In principle, a country could inflate its domestic economy without having to defend the existing exchange rate by buying its own currency. Instead, the falling currency would boost exports, further stimulating growth. However, as the case of France demonstrated, floating exchange rates in the context of international capital mobility made it increasingly difficult to reflate without setting off speculative runs on the currency. In this context, the collapse in 1983 of France's nationalist and Keynesian project served to redirect European capitalism toward a neoliberal economic strategy under the leadership of Jacques Delors, who, as Mitterrand's finance minister, had experienced the full force of international speculative attacks on the franc. The United States, however, remained a special case.

During the postwar era, US monetary and financial power was in large part a function of its industrial supremacy. After 1971, however, US power derived increasingly from the extraordinary ability of US financial institutions to create capital through credit and not simply or primarily through the accumulation of resources. As such traditional industries as steel and automotive declined, in part as a result of a geopolitical decision to remain open to Japanese (and, later, more generally, Asian) imports, the US government sought to establish liberal regimes in sectors it could dominate. These included pharmaceuticals, communication equipment, even agriculture, but in particular finance and financial services. Structural monetary and financial power has depended on national policies designed to make Wall Street the center of global credit, to impose an open door on the rest of the world to allow US access to domestic financial systems, and to eliminate barriers on the free flow of capital into the United States. These policies sprang from a logic that was as much political as economic or technological. The size and power of the US economy make it possible—in the context of floating exchange rates—to pursue economic policies according to the logic of domestic politics, a privilege that no single European country enjoys. This tendency has been reinforced by the progressive dominance of financial capital over industrial capital (van der Pijl, 1998: pp. 57–63; Duménil and Lévy, 2001: pp. 578–607). As Susan Strange has written, the deregulation of finance resulted from "certain specific political decisions or non-decisions taken by the leading financial authorities, especially in the United States" (1986: p. 60; see also Helleiner, 1994).

The dynamics of this structural power, rooted in finance but with profound implications for political and social relations in general, are accounted for admirably by Leonard Seabrooke (2001). The United States' structural power enables it to transform indebtedness into a strength by its ability to shape the preferences not only of debtors, but also of creditors. This has created a need to develop financial innovation, thereby enabling the United States essentially to tax the resources of the major holders of US debt in Asia (especially Japan, but in recent years also, notably, India and China) and Europe (especially Germany). Expansion of the euro-dollar market "provided a way of increasing the attractiveness of dollar holdings to foreigners" while facilitating the spread of off-shore financial markets. The United States "sought to avoid undertaking adjustment measures by encouraging foreign governments and private investors to finance these deficits" (Seabrooke, 2001: p. 10.; see also Gowan, 1999). In the 1980s, the United States began to attract massive capital inflows from the rest of the world. By 2006 the US current-account deficit had reached $869 billion. By the end of 2006, China held $345 billion in treasury securities and $1 trillion in currency, $700 million of which was in dollars (US Treasury, 2006).

Seabrooke's work is especially useful because of the clarity with which it spells out the broader politico-economic implications of its findings. His argument, then, deserves to be outlined in some detail. US structural financial and monetary power, while still institutionalized in the formal monetary regime, is exercised through a combination of "international passivity," "national activism," and "interactive embeddedness" of, inter alia, Washington politics, Wall Street "high finance," and the "main street" of US retail banking (2001: p. 19).

According to Seabrooke, the origins of US structural power derived from the advantages that the dollar's *numéraire* status gave US international banks in the Bretton Woods period. This offered these banks the opportunity to monopolize the issue of dollar-denominated liabilities with zero-exchange risk, which was subject to increased demand on the commercial loan, investment services, and foreign exchange markets due to the expansion of international trade (2001: p. 48). At the same time, and in sharp contrast to most European states, the more market-oriented Fordist settlement in the United States encouraged the development of a securitized domestic financial system (by encouraging "ordinary" people in the United States to invest in the stock market and to take on personal debt). Significantly, the US government created incentives for US banks to set up foreign subsidiaries, with measures designed in part to exercise control over domestic monetary policy despite the status of the dollar as a reserve currency, and in part to ensure US control over the emerging transnational financial networks.[4] As a result, US banks came to dominate the euro-dollar markets. These markets made it possible to expand dollar-denominated assets on a sufficient scale to facilitate international trade, without exerting adjustment constraints on the US economy (2001: pp. 64, 66–70).

This created the infrastructure that made it possible for the United States to exercise minimal hegemony when the Bretton Woods system collapsed. The uncertainties of exchange rates and interest rates favored the US economy both because the dollar remained the world's reserve currency and because the uncertainties promoted direct financing and, hence, the US economy, which had the "deepest" and most capitalized domestic financial market. Deep market capitalization also had a social base in the United States, which was lacking in the social compromises underpinning the Fordist welfare settlements in Europe.

Initially, US dominance was primarily derived from the dominant role of US banks in transatlantic arbitrage operations—an advantage that was multiplied by the oil crisis and the need to "recycle" the "petro-Dollars" (Seabrooke, 2001: pp. 73–106). However, the "indebted innovation" during the Reagan presidency added deeper structural dimensions to US power. While Washington initially considered regulating the euro-dollar market in 1978 amid concerns about the control of the domestic money supply, by the early 1980s—certainly by the time of Reagan's Economic Recovery Tax Act of 1981—it was decided that the best way to deal with the euro-dollar markets was to "internalize aspects of them within the US domestic financial system" (2001: p. 111). This internalization came in the form of a further commitment to highly capitalized, disintermediated, "direct-financing" capital markets as a way to deal with foreign exchange and interest rate uncertainties, and eventually also the debt crisis.

In the 1980s, financial innovation within the United States increased the capacity of the financial system to deal with higher levels of both personal and government debt. Money mutual funds expanded their operations. Futures trading on stock market indices started, and a broad range of options and derivatives were introduced. US commercial banks came to rely increasingly upon operations of debt securities (such as bonds and shares) rather than deposits ("off–balance-sheet activities"). Significantly, the 1984 Secondary Mortgage Market Enhancement Act created a market for mortgage-based securities. CMOs (Collateralized Mortgage Obligations) allowed "homeowners to draw against a line of credit supported by the appreciated value of their homes." In turn, commercial banks could sell the package of these loans to investment banks in order to create asset-backed securities, which would be sold as bonds to various investors as the basis for further investment ventures. Thus, increased home ownership provided investment banks with a steady supply of debt capital (Seabrooke, 2001: p. 118). Between 1980 and 1985, total US credit-market debt increased from $4.7 trillion to $8.2 trillion and non–financial sector debt increased from $3.9. trillion to $6.9 trillion. Household indebtedness increased by 69 percent. Most notably, this did not lead to economic stagnation. Rather, as suggested in the next chapter, it provided tremendous capacities for the United States to manipulate time and space as it restructured its capital accumulation regime along neoliberal, post-Fordist lines, backed up by military Keynesian stimulus (Harvey, 1990: pp. 182–183, 194–195). This highly capitalized market was also an attractive place for Japanese and European banks, given both the risks associated with the debt crisis, and exchange rate and interest rate volatility. In addition, Asian and European corporations were attracted to raising capital on the stock market as an alternative to their traditional house-bank links at home. Hence, when the US government sought ways to liberalize capital flows, for example through the yen-dollar agreement, they found ready allies within the business communities of their "opposite numbers."

Such agreements provided ways to finance the US balance-of-payment and government deficits. They also opened up new markets for the US financial services industry (Seabrooke, 2001: pp. 124–131). In this context, US assets are seen as less risky. From the large government deficits of the Reagan years to the massive explosion of private debt during Clinton's administration and to even greater governmental deficits under Bush II, capital accumulation has been sustained, despite relatively low yields on capital invested in the United States compared to the return of US investments abroad,[5] and despite the credit crises in Latin America, the former Communist states, and East Asia. Indeed, the US-centered system has managed to turn these crises into strengths by extending its control over—and progressively subsuming—disintegrated and weakened particularistic domestic systems (Grahl, 2001).

To be sure, as the 1987 stock-market crash and the ERM, "Tequila," Russian, and Asian credit crises in the 1990s demonstrated, there are systemic risks attached to a system that relies to such an extent on financial speculation. Nevertheless, at times of crisis central-bank trading networks and agreements on prudential supervision such as those under the Basle Accord have thus far proved sufficient to maintain the system. These accords have consistently been concluded to the advantage of US interests, supported by the United States' British allies, who have developed a niche strategy in the City of London to support this system (Seabrooke, 2001: pp. 131, 140). The US state intervenes in the real-estate market through "federally related mortgage pools" to underwrite credit risks (Duménil and Lévy, 2003: pp. 25–27). While certainly not without its

contradictions and limitations (to which we return, especially in the con-
cluding chapter), this system was, then, consolidated in the 1990s as the
remaining restrictions on banks engaging in direct financing were eliminated under the Clinton administration and when growth and productivity rates in the United States, in contrast to those in Japan and Europe,
were beginning to approximate the levels of the Fordist "golden age."

To sum up, at the national level, the United States has deregulated
its domestic financial markets in order to make them more competitive
internationally. The process of deregulation began in the 1960s with the
reopening of the City of London and the growth of the euro-dollar market. But a new wave began in the 1980s, culminating in the Financial
Services Modernization Act of 1998, which repealed the last vestiges of
New Deal legislation deriving from the Glass-Steagall Act. At the international level, the United States has resisted attempts to diminish the
role of the dollar, while also resisting capital controls and thereby pro-
moting the expansion of private capital in international finance. Through
its effective leadership of the IMF and World Bank, the United States has
blocked attempts to establish or maintain capital controls on a national
or regional basis, paving the way for the entry of US banks and financial corporations into Asian markets. The US Treasury used the Asian
financial crisis of 1997–1998 to restructure and liberalize the South
Korean economy, while blocking Japanese attempts to establish an
Asian Monetary Fund that would have reduced the role of the IMF and
undermined the Washington Consensus (Stiglitz, 2002: pp. 112–113;
Gowan, 1999: chap. 6; Wade, 2003).[6] As John Grahl writes (2005a:
p. 291),

> [T]he preponderance of the U.S. economy, far from giving way to
> competitive challenge, is greater than ever before. The capitalization
> of the two largest stock markets, NYSE and NASDAQ, for example,
> is some $11 trillion—half the world total. Similarly, dollar-denomi-
> nated securities constitute nearly half of the outstanding issues on
> world debt markets. Some 90 percent of recorded foreign exchange
> transactions involve the dollar. From the point of view of macroeco-
> nomic policy, this kind of scale does not so much limit as practically
> eliminate external financial constraints on the United States.

European Self-Limitation

During the Bretton Woods period, integral hegemony ensured international
support of the economic policies and terms of legitimacy of individual

European states. Western European countries "internalized" US monetary hegemony as they relied both on fixed exchange rates (to provide an anchor for the price system) and on external adjustment (to underwrite Keynesian strategies that supported their class compromises). In France, for example, the ability to devalue without serious short-term cost helped to create what Michael Loriaux (1991: pp. 10–11) calls the "overdraft economy," based on "the consensual refusal of the state, the trade unions, and the employers to control nominal changes in incomes and prices," unlimited credit, and the possibility of external adjustment. The inability to control credit produced a social compromise that automatically generated inflation and required periodic devaluations. Germany, by contrast, maintained a fixed but undervalued exchange rate of the mark to the dollar throughout the Bretton Woods period. This was consistent with its growth model, which depended on export-oriented growth based on competitive advantage in investment goods sectors, passive fiscal policy, and tight monetary policy, but strong unions in collective bargaining (Semmler, 1982).

However, the transition to floating exchange rates and mobile transnational financial markets under US tutelage, as outlined in the previous section, constituted a massive challenge. Whether monetary arrangements have been organized through the EMS or the EMU, the European single market operates within these structures, but from a radically different position of subordination, which results in a self-limitation on macroeconomic developments.

The failure of French Keynesianism under Mitterrand brought home the impasse of the overdraft economy. Subsequently, France has cooperated with neoliberal adjustment from a position of weakness within the second project of European integration, while in search for pan-European agreement to reconstitute the growth model (Clift, 2003: p. 179). Germany's dilemma was slightly different. In the early 1970s, the Schmidt administration was no longer willing to import US inflation via the fixed rates of the Bretton Woods agreement and therefore allowed the appreciation of the German mark, which in any case helped to contain the cost of oil imports. At the same time, floating exchange rates threatened to provoke competitive devaluations on a European level, and hence Germany began to search for fixed exchange rate agreements on German terms, in exchange for conditional support of other currencies through German foreign reserves (Lankowski, 1982: pp. 96–98).

Beginning in the early 1970s, the EU mounted a number of unsuccessful attempts to establish a "zone of stability" against the dollar. The Werner Plan of 1970 bore the imprint of German interest, viewing EMU as a means of reducing intra-European conflicts caused by French devaluation in the wake of 1968; but it also reflected Europe's resistance to US structural power, especially after the failure to impose an alternative international currency in the form of Special Drawing Rights on the United States (Parboni, 1982). The Basle Accord of 1972, the EMS, and the subsequent ERM all sought to maintain a system of internal fixed exchange rates.

Yet, these initiatives were undermined by Europe's collective vulnerability to US monetary unilateralism; chronic uneven development among the member states; and high levels of labor militancy, which made it impossible to maintain sufficient discipline or "internal adjustment" and thereby pass the burden of adjustment on to labor (Charchedi, 2001: pp. 145–156). Prior to EMU, the imbalance between Germany and the rest of the EU meant that the German mark was a powerful magnet for international capital seeking a safe and noninflationary haven. The 1992 collapse of the ERM, considered by the Bank of International Settlements to be the most significant international monetary crisis since the fall of the Bretton Woods system in 1971, exemplified this tendency (Seabrooke, 2001: p. 163). As long as European economies were expanding, ERM members were able to raise their interest rates in order to maintain parity with the rising mark. Reunification, however, precipitated a crisis (both for Germany and the EU as a whole) when the Bundesbank raised interest rates to unprecedented levels, ushering in a period of sustained economic stagnation in the fledgling single market.[7] In terms of broad socioeconomic trends, the EMS was a consistent drag on the stable expansion of aggregate demand and served to foreclose post-Fordist alternatives based on social-democratic and corporatist principles. The postunification boom and bust decisively ended a whole range of developments to that effect (Lipietz, 1989: pp. 37–50; 1997: pp. 1–41). Hence, the price for monetary integration has been sustained economic stagnation.

To be sure, the EMU was supposed to address the instabilities of the EMS. A common currency eliminates exchange rate risks and the need to hedge against such risks; the composition of the ECB also countered German unilateralism. However, as optimal currency area theory suggests, exchange rates are not only sources of instability for economic policy, but also shock absorbers. The abandonment of national currencies has served to displace the instabilities to other areas of economic policy. More fundamentally, the Maastricht design of the EMU amounts more to a continuation of the EMS regime than a fundamental break. As described above, it does not challenge the US-centered financial structures. If anything, the plethora of reforms of European financial systems is likely to con-solidate the subordinate convergence of European finance to these struc-tures (Story and Walter, 1997).[8]

EMU and Disciplinary Neoliberalism

The authority and terms of reference of the ECB, as laid down in the Treaty of Maastricht, also confirm the continuation of the principles of disciplinary neoliberal norms, new constitutional governance, and macro-economic austerity (Gill, 1998; Holman, 2004a). Since the launching of the euro on December 31, 1999, an "asymmetric and ECB-centered" (Dyson, 2000) project of economic regulation has been completed in the eurozone, with the key social purpose of this project being the institu-tionalization of "sound money." Central to this asymmetry is the cou-pling of a highly supranational and independent ECB with intergovern-mental arrangements in the fields of fiscal, labor-market, wage, and social policy. Furthermore, the governance of financial markets is strictly separated from macroeconomic policy and is confined to matters (such as prudential supervision) delegated to separate professional "apolitical" organizations (Padoa-Schioppa, 1997).

ECB independence is legally constituted in the Treaty of European Union (Articles 105 and 107), and can only be altered through a unani-mous decision by member states to alter the treaty. As a result, policymak-ing has become locked into this monetarist framework to an unprecedented degree. The treaty assigns to the ECB organizational independence from political processes to pursue its primary objective of price stability (TEU Articles 3a and 105[1]), as defined by the ECB itself. The ECB seeks to develop a policy that is "credible" in the financial markets, which in the end make the concrete decisions about the extension of liq-uidity and credit in the economy (Dyson, 2000). The Governing Coun-cil of the ECB is a highly supranational and cohesive entity; indeed, more so than the European Commission. It consists of six ECB execu-tive board members and the governors of the national central banks of the eurozone, who meet fortnightly. Formally, the threshold for decision is a simple majority vote, and each member is allocated only one vote. In practice, consensus decisions are sought, a process greatly facilitated by the professional sharing of the price stability paradigm and a clear mandate. It is clear that the board's mandate is to set a single monetary policy on the basis of data aggregated for the eurozone as a whole.[9]

Interest rate setting provides the ECB with a powerful bargaining tool vis-à-vis other organizations in the process of implicit policy coordination, especially in the fields of fiscal, wage, labor-market, and social policy. Policies that are contrary to the ECB's conception of price stability— and indirectly, it should be underlined, also productivity—are construed as entailing a higher risk of inflation, which in turn results in higher rates of interest. When policies pursued in these fields are not deemed to be credible by the ECB and financial markets, the price to pay is higher interest rates. The most important asymmetry is the one between a highly cohesive and supranational monetary policy and an intergovernmental fiscal policy. There is no meaningful EU budget and transfer-payment system available for an EU-wide "fiscal federalism"; to dispel any ambiguity on this point, the ECB is forbidden to lend directly to EU institutions and member states. (The Common Agricultural Policy [CAP] and regional policy funds, while important in specific sectors and regions, have little effect at an aggregate level.) Instead, the GSP has had the opposite effect. Constructed on the template of the initial Maastricht convergence criteria, the pact sought to preclude attempts by individual member states to "free ride on the policy credibility" of other states and EMU as a whole; that is, by pursuing expansionary fiscal policies without running the risk of a proportional rise of interest rates of the currency (as the effect would have been in the ERM). Especially important in this context was the 3 percent limitation of budget deficits. The Joint Coordination of National Employment Policies launched by the extraordinary Luxembourg Summit of 1997 has, through the "open method of coordination," become a benchmarking process emphasizing supply-side measures (deregulation) for employability. While its efficacy can be debated, as such it clearly is configured in the disciplinary neoliberal mold (Tidow, 2003). This also feeds into wage policy, which, in the context of a nonaccommodating macroeconomic policy, has forced European trade unions into concession bargaining in the form of "competitive corporatism" (Bieling and Schulten, 2003; Ryner and Schulten, 2003).

Permanent Crisis of the Eurozone

By permanently eliminating the depreciation option, EMU took the eurozone countries into turbulent and uncharted waters. The anti-inflationary precepts of the Bundesbank were carried over directly into the mandate of the ECB. The disciplinary and procyclical features of the GSP reflected the perceived interests of the stronger economies, most notably Germany's, in institutionalizing fiscal austerity through the aid of punitive measures. It is widely assumed that the imperatives of monetary union mean there is no alternative to Anglo-Saxon labor markets. This, however, presupposes that flexibilization is a solution, a presupposition that we challenge in the next chapter. As John Grahl has written, "If the stubborn search for flexibility, central to European economic policies for more than 20 years, could resolve the problem of unemployment in the EU it would have done so by now." Furthermore, there is no correlation between declines in real wages and investment: as a result of neoliberal measures, the share of wages in the EU GDP has declined significantly, while profit rates have increased substantially. These developments have failed to generate significant increases in investment (Grahl, 2005b: p. 2). As we explore further in the next chapter, the result is a vicious circle of restrictive monetary policies, rising unemployment, and a decrease of actual and potential growth. Finally, the euro-zone is not an optimal currency area (Eichengreen, 1992), which is a significant problem in the absence of a system of fiscal federalism. The resulting problems of uneven development exacerbate conflicts and preempt consolidation of common action for "positive integration."

The eurozone, then, lacks the necessary cultural and political foundations for stability. The EU has no centralized fiscal policy and, as the history of the GSP made clear, over the long haul no intergovernmental pact can compensate for the absence of a genuine polity. The pact demanded steep cuts in social spending throughout the Union, but low growth has placed severe pressure on national budgets. The absence of a sizeable Union budget does not allow for the extensive redistributive policies necessary to minimize uneven development by compensating weaker economies that have lost the option of devaluation. Instead, uneven development tends to foment nationalism, as strong political and cultural units are inevitably pitted against an unaccountable central bank that has been forced to bear the entire burden of macroeconomic management (De Grauwe, 2006c).

Given the structural limitations of the eurozone and the monetarist straitjacket of the ECB, it is easy to see in retrospect that slow growth would eventually force governments to face the implications of the one-sided nature of the GSP and then effectively tear it up in November 2003, as they sought to reassert control over the policy instruments still available to them. Italy provides the clearest example of the limitations of the eurozone. Throughout the postwar period, depreciation of the lira served to compensate for Italy's lack of competitiveness, although it generated increasing public debt and inflation and provided no external mechanism to limit wage increases. In 1993 the departure from the ERM and a 34 percent devaluation led to an export boom. Conformity to the Maastricht criteria and accession to EMU were to provide a "self-binding" mechanism, or *vincolo esterno,* bringing public finances and inflation under control (Giavazzi and Pagano, 1990). However, Italy has experienced significant declines in relative productivity. Between 1995 and 2003, Italy experienced the second-lowest growth rate within the eurozone as it pursued, first, radical austerity to qualify for inclusion and, then, between 1999 and 2002, remained within the terms of the GSP. Finally, in 2003 Italy abrogated its commitments in the context of public debt equal to 117 percent of GDP (Posen, 2005a: p. 134). While calls for a return to the lira reflected domestic electoral calculations and overlooked the considerable political and financial costs of such a dramatic step, they nevertheless indicate the depth of the crisis in Italy.

By 2003 it was widely recognized that the GSP not only was placing excessive pressure on weaker economies, but also no longer accorded with the interest of stronger economies, including those of Germany and France. In Germany, despite substantial structural reform of labor markets, unemployment increased from 4.5 percent in 1992 to 11 percent in 2005, before falling back to under 9 percent in 2007. Facing a similar dilemma, France joined with Germany in November 2003 to render the pact inoperative. The agreement to "relax enforcement procedures" was in fact an acknowledgment of its demise.

The Economic and Financial Affairs Council (ECOFIN) reached an agreement to "amend" the pact on March 21, 2005 (Council of the EU, 2005; European Commission, 2005a and 2005b). While being presented as an improvement, the amendments undoubtedly represent a radical retraction of the objectives initially set for the GSP. They represent a belated admission of the trade-off between macroeconomic "balance" in the medium term and growth (which we discuss in Chapter 3). As such, the amended pact is often represented as more "intelligent" than the previous version. But it is questionable whether the amended pact can be considered a "pact" at all. The amended GSP is full of general clauses, inviting ad hoc, arbitrary, and discretionary interpretations. First, the call for a differentiated assessment of Medium Term Objectives (in light of structural policies pursued and potential growth rates) opens up considerable room for interpretation, disagreement, and conflict. The same is the case for "exceptional" and "temporary" deficits "close" to the reference value. But the most notable general clause is the one stating that "due consideration will be given *to any other factors, which in the opinion of the nation state concerned* are relevant in order to comprehensively assess in qualitative terms the excess over the reference value. In that context, *special consideration will be given to budgetary efforts towards increasing, or maintaining at a high level, financial contributions, international solidarity and to achieving European policy goals, notably the unification of Europe* if it has a detrimental effect on the growth of fiscal burden of a Member State" (Council of the EU, 2005: p. 15 [our italics]). The last contains considerable ambiguity. It should be seen against the backdrop of Germany's invocation of its exceptional burden of financing German reunification and France's invocation of its expenditure on defense as a contribution to the Common Foreign and Security Policy (CFSP) during the negotiations leading up to the amendments. During these negotiations, according to Euro-12 Chairman Jean-Claude Juncker, "[V]iews were expressed . . . with a vehemence that amazed me" (Parker, 2005; *Financial Times,* 2005a).

While the euro is not immediately dependent on the GSP in the short term, uncertainties over fiscal policy have the potential to erode its credibility in the eyes of financial markets over the longer term. For the time being, the issue hinges on the question of the spread of bond yields. Questions are being raised over whether the ECB is artificially supporting bonds issued by member states with a low credit rating in order to minimize spreads and turbulence—which would increase the demand for hedging that the monetary union was supposed to eliminate (e.g., Atkins, 2006). In any case, the ECB acknowledges that bond and other financial markets are insufficient corrective mechanisms to sustain investors' confidence in public finances, and in this context increased variations in macroeconomic policies remain a source of centrifugal effects that strain the monetary union (Atkins, 2006). Alternatively, member states might nevertheless seek to pursue fiscal discipline in accordance with the original pact, notwithstanding the weakening of the language. However, as argued in Chapters 3 and 4, the likely consequences of this would be an accentuation of the internal pressures that drive member states to abandon their pact commitments. When this happens, it will not help that the common perception now exists that the inconsistent application of the pact does not reflect general multilateral norms, but rather the particular interests of the two largest member states of the monetary union.

Faced with this "fiscal rebellion," the ECB renews its commitments to price stability at all costs. The mantra of "structural reforms" is invoked to save the single currency (OECD, 2007). We contend in Chapters 3 and 4 that these policies not only generate increasing national and regional political instability, but also are counterproductive in their own terms.

Global Limitations of the Euro

The foregoing suggests why, in view of the claims and predictions that EMU presents a fundamental challenge to US hegemony, and, given the overall context of aggressive assertion of US financial interests in the 1990s, the US response toward EMU has been rather muted. US official and semi-official commentary with respect to the euro during the 1990s, in fact, replicated the response toward the single market a decade earlier. At the outset of the single-market program, there was substantial opposition in Washington to an anticipated French model of "fortress Europe," which had the potential to exclude US capital and trade. When it became clear by the early 1990s that the single market would, in reality, reflect an Anglo-German preference for Atlantic economic integration, opposition evaporated.[10] To be sure, Washington's attitude of benign neglect has had numerous proximate causes, including widespread scepticism prior to 1999 resulting from the EMU's political and structural limitations (Posen, 2005a) and Britain's refusal to join the eurozone. More fundamentally, however, the monetary union as presently constituted is subordinated to the US policy of financial liberalization and, as we argue in Chapter 5, is inextricably linked to broader US geopolitical hegemony.

Although the prospect of monetary union does not appear to have produced widespread alarm on Wall Street or in Washington, there are nevertheless two significant long-term sources of US concern. The first is the protectionist potential of EMU. Between its launch in 1999 and the spring of 2002, the euro declined by 25 percent against the dollar. A number of factors can be cited to account for this decline, including the position of financial markets toward a new and uncertain currency. However, there is also evidence that during the period 1999–2001 the ECB sought to accommodate EU export interests and to moderate the conflicts arising from tight fiscal policies (Talani, 2005, 2006; Campanella, 2002). What amounts to a form of covert "neoliberal mercantilism" highlights the contradictions and limitations of the monetary union. It suggests that the ECB is willing at times to navigate between the particular national interests of strong states (or, at least, the interests of their export-oriented capitalists) and the viability of the euro as a global currency.

Second, much of the commentary in congressional and academic circles has focused on the issue of seignorage and the possibility that the euro will reduce this benefit to the United States. However, although the euro will certainly displace the dollar in some areas, especially in central and eastern Europe, it is doubtful that, in the absence of a more generalized global economic crisis, the overall impact would be large enough to constitute a major challenge to the dollar. It has been argued, moreover, that the underlying fragility of the dollar, in view of US budget and trade deficits and dependency on foreign capital, will at some point induce investors and governments to rebalance their portfolios and thereby establish the euro as a rival currency. Yet, the crippling political limitations on the eurozone, dramatized by the rejection of the Constitutional Treaty and the growth of economic nationalism, do not bode well for the emergence of the euro as a rival to the dollar (Cohen, 2003). Although virtually all central banks are moving to diversify reserves, this is unlikely to involve a wholesale shift away from the dollar that would endanger its status as reserve currency.

Europe remains heavily dependent on the United States in terms both of trade and investment and of the ripple effects of US macroeconomic policies. Transatlantic economic integration has accelerated dramatically over the last twenty-five years. Almost two-thirds of foreign investment controlled by EU firms goes to the United States. The United States absorbs 20 to 25 percent of European exports (Quinlan, 2003) while US consumer spending continues to account for 20 percent of global economic activity (Gross, 2007, P. D4) and global exports (Roach, 2007). The United States is expected in the period 2006–2010 to maintain its position as primary destination for foreign direct investment (Economist Intelligence Unit, 2006). Warnings of coming trade wars in the business press, based on conflicts in highly visible sectors such as agriculture, aircraft, and steel, greatly underestimate the generally high degree of openness and absence of friction in transatlantic trade, 95 percent of which is subject to no barriers whatsoever (Hufbauer and Neumann, 2002; Cafruny, 2002). The centerpiece of the German European Council presidency in 2007 is the establishment of a transatlantic free-trade zone. And the speed and intensity with which developments in US financial markets impact the rest of the world underscore Europe's continuing dependence on Washington and Wall Street (Munchau, 2007: p. 12).

These considerations suggest that the claim of transatlantic "decoupling" that has accompanied Europe's modest post-2005 recovery is premature. Through its structural power, the United States has thus far been able to resolve problems and contradictions arising from massive trade deficits, chronically low savings, and continuing dependency on inflows of foreign capital. To be sure, the global financial system is displaying signs of growing instability. Yet, notwithstanding the travails of the dollar, a topic we return to in Chapter 5, neoliberal Europe has not emerged from the shadow of minimal US hegemony.

Conclusion

After a section that defined some of the central concepts used, this chapter has explained the central dynamics and mechanisms through which the EMU is an institutional expression of European subordination to US structural power, as configured primarily through financial markets. Since the collapse of the Bretton Woods system, Washington and Wall Street have pursued a set of increasingly predatory policies that have allowed the United States to achieve sustained growth. By contrast, Europe's policies have resulted in self-limitation as described in the last section of this chapter.

It is important to underline that the "success" of US economic policy, as outlined above, is an outcome of structural power and not systems superiority in any straightforward functional sense. Even on such a narrow economic criterion as maximization of profit on invested capital, as we have seen, the yield of foreign capital invested in the United States is comparatively low. Furthermore, it is highly questionable whether the US model represents a superior system of technological innovation (beyond strictly financial innovation) compared to such systems that facilitated the development of Japanese and German export competitiveness in manufacturing trade. It rather seems to lead to low rates of investment in productive capital and technological innovation, and to an increasingly skewed income distribution in favor of the very rich who exercise strategic control over capital (Duménil and Lévy, 2001; 2004). (And, notwithstanding the degree to which large strata of the US middle classes are involved in the financial system, strategic control of their assets is exercised by a small group of institutional investors.)

Nevertheless, it is no doubt the performance of the United States in the 1980s and 1990s that European elites seek to emulate through EMU and the deregulation of financial services. However, the European strategy disregards the entrenched position that US investors maintain global markets, buttressed by the continuing seignorage status of the dollar. It also underestimates the degree to which US structural power is based on the social integration of global finance into the US financial market segmentation, transforming hitherto highly successful national systems of innovation, and commodifying institutions such as pension funds that reflect deeply embedded class compromises. Hence, whereas the United States has been able to draw on global finance and its "interactive embeddedness" with Washington, Wall Street, and "Main Street" to turn credit into capital, in Europe deregulation and neoliberal economic policies as entrenched in the EMU have progressively led to a self-limiting subordination to global finance.

Notes

1. This analysis is heavily influenced by Nicos Poulantzas (1974: pp. 145–179). Partly influenced by Jean-Jacques Servan-Schreiber's *The American Challenge* (1969, published in French in 1967), Poulantzas assigned central importance to the manner in which US foreign direct investments (FDI) in Europe directly influenced the social organization of production. This was for him not only an issue of aggregate direct US ownership, but of the manner in which US ownership and control were concentrated in leading sectors, standardizing base materials and making European capital dependent on these. He also emphasized the then-nascent importance of US investment banking for the finance of European capital. In retrospect, Poulantzas overestimated the effect of FDI through US transnational corporations (TNCs), but, as we will discuss below, the role of US finance in the direct structuring of European capital would become more important. According to Poulantzas, this "displaced" the modus operandi and paradigm of practices ("ideology," in his broad and materialist sense of the term) of European capital toward US capital, both through a subordination via property relations and through an increased managerial control. Hence, although transnational European capital retained its own autonomy (and as such was not similar in status to, say, the Latin American "comprador bourgeoisie"), it was increasingly intertwined, by multiple links of dependence, to US capital. This, according to Poulantzas, accentuated the contradictions between European transnational capital and compromised interclass mediation and reproduction functions of European states. European transnational capital was losing its autonomy in the political and ideological fields, and was thus progressively alienated from the specific terms of Europe's distinct social accords (pp. 165–170).

2. See van Apeldoorn (2002) and Bieling (2003). This has served the profitability and merger objectives of European business. See European Commission (1996).

3. We are aware that there is debate in the literature we cite concerning which of these factors is the primary one; and which one is cause and which one effect. Since we are primarily concerned with the implications of the exhaustion of Fordism, we do not comment on this debate here.

4. Seabrooke (2001) mentions the 1963/64 Interest Equalization Tax (IET), the 1965 Voluntary Foreign Credit Restraint Program (VFCR), and the Foreign Direct Investment Program (FDIP) of the same year to be of particular importance. The VFCR curbed borrowing of foreign firms on US domestic financial markets and the FDIP restrained the amount that US firms could send abroad. However, most importantly, the regulations *did not apply to foreign subsidiaries of US banks* (p. 60).

5. Processing data from the French state and the Federal Reserve, Duménil and Lévy (2003: pp. 664–665) show that yields on US direct investments abroad are about three times larger than the yields on foreign direct investments in the United States. With regard to total holdings, the yield on the holdings of the United States in the rest of the world is more than twice that on the holdings of the rest of the world in the United States. Consistent with our argument, they attribute this asymmetry to the United States' being "at the center of a system in which capital is simultaneously exported and imported, to and from the rest of the world. . . . Agents of other countries may want to protect their holdings

from national risk or constraints. . . . Such investments are seen as risk free and liquid, but are remunerated at comparatively low rates" (p. 665).

6. During 2006, the center of gravity in international financial markets began noticeably to shift away from New York toward London and, to a lesser extent, toward Hong Kong and Dubai. This shift in no way represents a challenge to the United States' structural financial power and the underlying global financial regime. The growth of competing financial sectors is a form of outsourcing that has been led by US banks such as Goldman, Morgan Stanley, Merrill Lynch, and Lehman Brothers, whose international revenues from corporate and investment banking in Europe and Asia are outstripping those of their US business. It reflects the drive toward competitive deregulation and competitive tax cutting in the global financial sector, as US banks seek to overturn post-Enron regulations, such as Sarbanes-Oxley, and gravitate toward London, which has always dominated the global foreign-exchange market. It has been accompanied by the New York Stock Exchange's purchase of Euronext and NASDAQ's move on the London Stock Exchange. The growth of London is also a reflection of the deepening of "Anglo-Saxon" corporate practices in Europe, as companies that have traditionally relied on commercial banks are turning to capital markets (see, for example, Callaway, 2006: p. 6; Wighton and White, 2007: p. 1; Tett, 2007: p. 26).

7. This was due to the combination of the tight monetary policy of the Bundesbank and the expansionary fiscal policy resulting from Kohl's election promises to the East. The cost of reunification represented 5.5 percent of Germany's annual GNP and resulted in a serious budget shortfall. This was compounded by promises to establish a 1:1 parity with the Ostmark and not to increase taxes to fund unification. The policy stance of the reunifying Germany has definite parallels with that of the United States toward the rest of the world in the 1980s; however, without the depth in domestic securities markets or coordinated industrial policy to be able to use this policy stance to facilitate sustained internal capital accumulation. At the same time as the ERM crisis gathered momentum, the US Federal Reserve cut interest rates, a decision France called an "Anglo Saxon plot to undermine the movement toward European unity" (quoted in Seabrooke, 2001: p. 163). Despite spending half of its reserves to buy pounds and despite, as well, a five-point increase in interest rates on September 16, 1992 ("Black Wednesday"), Britain was forced to exit the ERM. After similar massive and costly intervention, Italy followed suit. Speculation against the franc during the summer of 1993 necessitated the widening of ERM margins of fluctuation to 30 percent, as the EMU appeared headed for disaster. Between September 1992 and March 1995, the lira fell by 35 percent against the mark, the peseta dropped 29 percent, and the pound lost 19 percent of its value. The EMU project survived the attendant turbulence, albeit, significantly, without Britain, which rather pursues a national strategy anchored to the United States, given the role of the City of London in US-led financial markets.

8. There is, of course, a voluminous literature on the causal chain of decisionmaking that led to EMU. Scholars have pointed variously to the power-political context of the Franco-German axis (e.g., Andrews, 1993; Baun, 1996; Moravcsik, 1998) and US-European rivalry (Feldstein, 1997; Ross, 2004; Dyson and Featherstone, 1999); the influence of interest groups and class fractions

(e.g., Frieden, 1991; Talani, 2003); and the role of ideas (e.g., McNamara, 1998). Our analysis of US structural power and the subordinate role of European capital in the impact of EMU (and EMS) is fully in accord with accounts that stress the desire of governments to elicit domestic austerity with reference to binding supranational agreements (e.g., Gill, 1998; Giavazzi and Pagano, 1988; Pierson, 1996; Ross, 2004). Rawi Abdelal usefully points to the leadership role of French and European officials, who were far more interested than their US counterparts in promulgating multilateral rules of neoliberal globalization of finance in the EU as well as in the OECD and IMF. However, only by overlooking the national and transatlantic structural constraints operating on these officials is it possible to claim that, with respect to these rules, the United States was "irrelevant, inconsequential, and indifferent" and that "Europe did not capitulate to global capital" (Abdelal, 2006: p. 1).

9. Possible limitations to this supranationalist quality of the ECB include the facts that the national central bankers make up the majority and that the national central banks are shareholders rather than subsidiaries of the ECB. Furthermore, operational aspects of monetary policy have remained at the level of national central banks. These include the right to conduct money-market operations and the regulation and supervision of their respective domestic financial markets. At the same time, the centrifugal effects of this should not be exaggerated, as the monetary policy mandate is quite clear and as specialized professionals share a similar outlook. The terms of disagreement of central bankers is rather narrow (Dyson, 2000: pp. 23–24).

10. The most prominent US sceptic was Martin Feldstein (1997, p. 60), who warned, "If EMU does come into existence . . . it will change the political character of Europe in ways that could lead to conflicts in Europe and confrontations with the United States."

3

The Failed Takeoff of a "New Economy"

Sometimes it is hard to escape the thought that the single-minded focus on the labor market stems from the naïve belief that unemployment must be a defect in the labor market, as if the hole in a flat tyre must always be at the bottom, because that is where the tyre is flat.
—Robert Solow (2000: p. 7)

Europe needs a process in which all sectors which fail to liberalize and open up to competition are subject to independent investigation and enforcement, undertaken free from national political interference.
—(United Kingdom, HM Treasury, 2006: p. 10)

In the latter half of the 1990s, the term *new economy* became popular as a shorthand way to describe the rather surprisingly strong and sustained pattern of noninflationary growth in the United States (e.g., Kelly, 1998). With an average annual real GDP growth rate of 4.1 percent during the latter part of that decade, US growth almost matched the 4.4 percent mark of the "golden age" between 1960 and 1973. By contrast, average annual real GDP growth during this period in the fledgling eurozone remained sluggish at 2.7 percent. Thus it did not much improve on the figures of the stagflation decade of the 1970s, which had ushered in the "crisis of Keynesianism," or in the 1980s. While US growth figures tailed off between 2000 and 2005 (taking off some of the hubristic edge of the "new economy" notion), at an annual average of 3.1 percent they remained well above anything that the eurozone had mustered since the early 1970s. In the same time period, the eurozone recorded an abysmal average annual growth rate of 1.4 percent (Figure 3.1).

Figure 3.1 Average Annual Real Growth of GDP, United States and the Eurozone

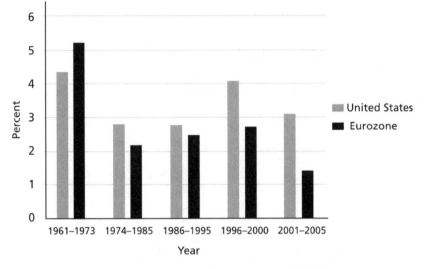

Source: European Commission (2006a: Statistical Annex, pp. 196, 215).

The strict monetary policy regime continued to maintain low inflation rates on both sides of the Atlantic. But, by contrast, a notable performance gap also appeared in productivity. It should be acknowledged that nothing has been able to compare with European productivity growth during the catch-up phase of post–World War II reconstruction.[1] In addition, while US labor productivity is beginning to reach the levels of the golden age, the same cannot be said for total factor productivity.[2] Nevertheless, between 1994 and 2003 European productivity levels fell from 94 to 85 percent of US levels. This represents one-fifth of the European catch-up during the previous half century (Gordon, 2004: Tables 1 and 2) and is reflected in a number of different measures of productivity growth (Figure 3.2). With average annual labor-productivity growth at 0.8 percent and total factor productivity growth at 0.2 percent, European performance was especially abysmal during the first five years of the twenty-first century.

These economic indicators were disappointing almost a decade and a half after 1992, the year when the Single European Market project (SEM) was completed and when the commitment to the EMU was made through the Maastricht Treaty ratification process. After all, ensuring a European economic dynamism that was not fundamentally dependent on the United States had been the central objective of the "re-launch" of European integration (Sandholtz and Zysman, 1989). Actual growth figures were totally

Figure 3.2 Average Annual Real Productivity Growth, United States and the Eurozone

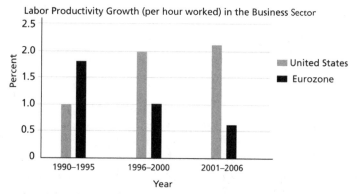

Source: Organisation for Economic Co-operation and Development (2006a: Annex Table 12).

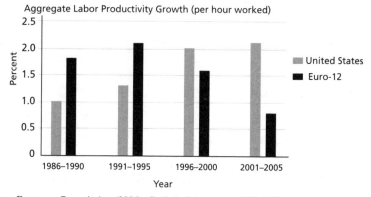

Source: European Commission (2006a: Statistical Annex, pp. 196, 215).

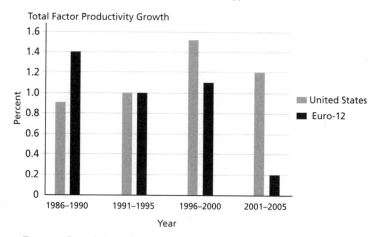

Source: European Commission (2006a: Statistical Annex, pp. 196, 215).

out of step with the rosy scenario painted by the Cecchini Report, which had estimated "a cumulative impact" of +4.5 to 7 percent on GDP of the SEM in a five- to six-year period after completion and a net increase of at least two million jobs (Emerson, Aujean, Catinat, Goybet, and Jaquemin, 1988: pp. 5–6).

Not surprisingly, disappointing figures for the unemployment rate have been a corollary to the disappointing figures in growth. Unemployment increased from already high levels during the Maastricht convergence process; subsequently, it has consistently been 3.5 to 5 percent above that of the United States (Figure 3.3). In addition, while the employment rate in the eurozone has increased somewhat in recent years (reflecting both a change toward "activation" in unemployment insurance and employment policy and an increase in the female participation rate), at 65.5 percent in 2005, it remained well below the 71.2 percent rate in the United States (Organisation for Economic Co-operation and Development, 2006: Annex Table 20).

The EU has responded to these disappointments with more of the same. Making explicit reference to the notion "new economy," the so-called Lisbon process that was launched in 2000 famously aims to turn the SEM into "the most competitive and dynamic knowledge-based economy in the world" by 2010 (European Council, 2000). To the same

Figure 3.3 Unemployment Rates, United States and the Eurozone

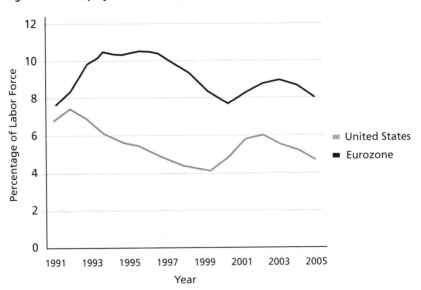

Source: Organisation for Economic Co-operation and Development (2004; 2006: Annex, Table 13).

objective, the Cardiff process promised further efforts to implement reforms (notably in the financial services industry), which resulted in the Financial Services Action Plan (FSAP). The premise behind the Lisbon and Cardiff processes is not that the disappointments so far indicate that there is something wrong in the assumptions behind the SEM and the EMU, but, rather, that the problem is one of inadequate implementation. In other words, the deregulatory "bonfire of controls" of the SEM and the monetarist macroeconomic discipline of the EMU should now be complemented with a surveillance and benchmarking process with performance targets, ensuring that "best practice" is disseminated throughout the Union in an "open method of coordination."[3]

The EU sticks to the rationale set out in the Cecchini Report: the removal of artificial internal barriers to trade will ensure a more optimal division of labor and allocation of scarce resources via competition. Dynamic economies, in the form of economies of scale, technological development, and diffusion are understood exclusively as effects of these static economies of allocation (Emerson, Aujean, Catinat, Goybet, and Jaquemin, 1988; European Commission, 1993). The case for the EMU is presented as a variant of this argument. The irrevocable fixing of exchange rates removes uncertainties that are hindering the deepening of the SEM. The result of fixing exchange rates is the reduction of transaction costs, which further removes barriers to trade and increases rates of profit. The independence of the ECB and the excessive deficit clause of the GSP increase the credibility of the common currency in free, and therefore efficient, financial markets. The attendant lower rates of interest, together with high profits in a context of competition, produce a higher rate of welfare-generating investments. These are further induced by the deregulation of labor markets and the tax and welfare systems that result from the tightening of macroeconomic constraints. The outcome of this is a more flexible and mobile labor force, which can be better deployed with the new investments. The overall result is a new EU dynamism: more innovation, faster growth, more employment, higher profitability, and, in time, higher real wages; in short, Pareto optimality (European Commission, 1990). As ECB chief economist Otmar Issing writes (2002: pp. 345–346), and quite consistently with what we call "asymmetrical regulation" in the previous chapter,

> [T]here are no convincing arguments in favour of attempts to co-ordinate macroeconomic policy *ex ante* in order to achieve an overall policy mix favourable to growth and employment. On the contrary, [such attempts] give rise to the risk of confusing the specific roles, mandates and responsibilities of the policies in question. They thereby reduce the transparency of the overall economic policy framework for the

general public, and tend to prevent the individual policy makers from being held accountable. Instead I . . . argue that national governments and autonomous social partners should design and implement the policies for which they are responsible, bearing in mind the overall stability framework provided for in the Maastricht Treaty and the secondary legislation, including the stability and growth pact. . . . Obviously, if national governments and social partners take the single monetary policy's credible commitment to maintain price stability as given, when deciding their own actions, this will lead to *implicitly* co-ordinated policy outcomes *ex post,* while at the same time limiting policy conflicts and overall economic uncertainty.

In this chapter we posit that rather than sticking to this mode of analysis in the face of overwhelming evidence to the contrary, there are strong reasons to doubt the two central points upon which this argument rests: namely, first, that active monetary policy *ex ante* is at best neutral and at worst counterproductive; and, second, that the key to unleashing a new economy dynamism in Europe is the dismantling of welfare systems that are held to be distorting the labor market. Rather, the failure to launch the SEM into a dynamic new economic trajectory has to do with what we have identified, in the previous chapter, as the self-limiting nature of the EMU. That is, a straitjacket has been put on monetary and fiscal policy, which has resulted in an internal European "game" of competitive austerity, which Albo (1994) defines as

[a situation in which] each country reduces domestic demand and adopts an export-oriented strategy of dumping its surplus production [by keeping wages below productivity growth and pushing down domestic costs], for which there are fewer consumers in its national economy. (p. 147)

This is in sharp contrast to the US case, where external borrowing has served to underpin output and, to some extent, productivity growth.

Sources of European Stagnation: "Eurosclerosis," "Baumolitis," or Uneven and Sluggish Growth in Aggregate Demand?

The framework outlined by Issing is not a viable basis for a self-sustaining, dynamic, regional European economy. Apart from making the standard monetarist assumption of a radical separation between the "monetary" and "real" economies, which is contradicted by ECB practice itself,[4] Issing, along with the conventional Euro-wisdom he represents, commits a fallacy of composition. He extrapolates from the particular export-oriented niche strategy of the so-called German model of the late 1970s and the 1980s—the strategy of accommodation by a mid-range power to the US predatory minimal hegemony of the late 1970s and the 1980s. This is a strategy that could only work in particular circumstances, and these circumstances no longer obtain in Germany itself. Deregulation of welfare systems, the favored response to these changing conditions, is neither a necessary nor sufficient solution in this context. Apart from failing to reignite growth, this policy is also failing to achieve the Walrasian equilibrium and Pareto optimality of which liberal idealists dream. Rather, the policy undermines the institutional framework that embeds the social market economies. The result is profound social dislocations that, as will be demonstrated in the next two chapters, threaten political stability and the vitality of European democracy itself.

Competitive austerity can be interpreted, then, as, an external side effect of the US minimal hegemony described in the previous chapter; a side effect born in Europe at high social and economic costs. Paradoxically, insofar as the EU insists on more of the same, in ever wider spheres of social activity, the effect of competitive austerity has been a deepening of the ideological aspects of this hegemony, at least among European elites. To point to the ideological nature of the current pattern of economic restructuring in Europe is not, however, to suggest that it would be easy to reverse once the ideological blinds are removed. Even if a wider range of European interests would be served through an alternative concept of economic governance, collective action problems create tremendous obstacles for any attempt to change the current pattern. It is not suggested here that no interests are served in Europe by the prevailing pattern. Rather, competitive austerity is a zero-sum game of winners and losers. As discussed in the previous chapter, this is, in particular, the case both with European export-oriented big business, which enjoys high rates of profit despite the sluggishness of the European economy as a whole, and with certain privileged core-regions and social strata that sometimes constitute the political majority of complete member states (such as Luxembourg, Ireland, the Netherlands in the 1990s, and the Scandinavian countries since the late 1990s). Furthermore, politically important regions and strata in some previously underdeveloped regions (such as Ireland, parts of Spain and Portugal, and even parts of eastern Europe) are relatively better off as a result of the SEM and the EMU. These winners, who can be seen as constituent parts of a US-centered, neoliberal "organic alliance," have sufficient weight in EU institutions to exert a veto over any reform to the EMU. However, at the same time, large segments that previously were part of the organic alliance are increasingly marginalized, not least in the Franco-German core, and this is a source of emergent crisis tendencies.

Eurosclerosis and Baumolitis?

Of course, attributing European stagnation to the demand-side effects of EMU-induced austerity is not uncontroversial. The overwhelming mainstream consensus is rather that it is supply-side constraints—diseconomies generated from market-distorting welfare and labor-market policies, often referred to as "eurosclerosis"—that, in the last instance, account for European stagnation. Insofar as the demand side enters, it is seen as epiphenomenal to supply-side factors.

To make our argument convincing, it is necessary to confront the widely held assumption that the imperatives of monetary union mean there is no alternative to the adoption of Anglo-Saxon models of deregulated labor markets, product markets, and the removal of other barriers to competition. Reform in this direction is seen as necessary to boost employment, output, and productivity growth and to reduce instability associated with the risks of asymmetric shocks (intimately related to what we call "uneven development") in what might not immediately be an "optimal currency area" (e.g., De Grauwe, 2003).

It should also be pointed out that in recent years many of those who were the most influential proponents of Europe's variety of capitalism, and who celebrated the positive externalities of codetermination, labor-market policies, and stability induced by corporatist bargaining (which generated highly competitive "diversified quality production" and competitiveness in world markets, at the same time as it generated social cohesion), have joined the eurosclerosis chorus (e.g., Esping-Andersen, 1996; Streeck and Trampusch, 2005). This has resulted in the virtual disappearance of an alternative and heterodox view to the mainstream eurosclerosis thesis.

This can largely be explained with reference to what is believed to be the nature of the "service sector," which has been the main source of employment growth over the past twenty-five years. Whereas it might be possible to develop a high-wage economy with a generous welfare state on the basis of diversified quality production in an economy where output and employment are principally based on manufacturing, this is not possible (according to this view) when technological advances dictate that the main avenue for employment expansion is provided by, as is the case now, the service sector (due to the high degree of capital intensity in manufacturing). This view is given empirical credibility by the fact that service-driven employment growth has been strong in economies with deregulated labor markets, such as the economies of the United States and the United Kingdom. Theoretically, the view seems to rest on what at first glance is a simply stated, yet compelling, 1967 hypothesis attributed to Baumol (Pierson, 2001). According to this account, the problems that the European social model faces can be reduced to the very nature of service production. In contrast to manufacturing, qua the Fordist model, service production cannot yield the continuous productivity growth that previously made it possible to grant both high profits and social wages. It is simply not possible to increase, say, childcare provision, catering, or legal advice in this way. As a result, employment expansion in a "postindustrial" economy depends on wages and benefits adjusting to the diminishing returns of output expansion that are inherent in the service sector. Such adjustment is possible in the flexible Anglo-Saxon markets, but not in the European social market economies, where high wages and benefits form barriers of entry for service production. Consequently, these economies are seen as suffering from "Baumolitis," where a highly capital-intensive and, to be sure, competitive manufacturing sector is not flanked by a service sector that can absorb surplus labor. The result is a vicious circle, where payroll surcharges have to increase to meet unemployment insurance commitments, rendering wage costs even higher.

However, despite the widespread acceptance of these assumptions, the empirical evidence behind them is surprisingly unimpressive. First, the correlation between deregulated labor markets and employment is very weak (Organisation for Economic Co-operation and Development, 2000; Buchele and Christiansen, 1998; Glyn, 2001; Eurostat, 2001; Goul Andersen, 2007). Disaggregating the data somewhat further and observing paradigmatic cases of different types of welfare states provide further evidence that, despite the elegance and parsimony of the eurosclerosis cum Baumolitis thesis, it does not hold water.

Table 3.1 compares what the Baumolitis thesis would theoretically predict with empirical evidence that rather clearly exposes its hypothetical axioms as false. Theoretically, the United States, as the paradigmatic case of a liberal welfare state with few restrictions to the free operation of the labor market, represents an economy that has adjusted to postindustrialism. To be sure, productivity growth is no longer likely

Table 3.1 Postindustrialism in Different Types of Welfare States: Hypothesis vs. Empirics

	United States (Liberal)	Germany (Christian Democratic)	Sweden (Social Democratic)
Employment Rate	High	Low	High
Unemployment Rate	Low	High	Low
Labor Productivity Growth, Predicted	Low	High	Low
Output Growth, Predicted	High	Low	Low
Inflation	Low	Low	High
Budget Balance	Balance	Balance	Deficit
Employment Rate[a]	73.1	68.5	71.9
Unemployment Rate[b]	5.0	8.0	5.7
Labor Productivity Growth[c]	2.1	1.8	2.2
Output Growth[d]	3.2	1.3	2.7
Rate of Inflation[e]	2.1	0.6	1.3
Government Balance[f]	−2.2	−3.9	+1.3

Source: European Commission (2006a) Statistical Annex; Organisation for Economic Cooperation and Development (2006): Statistical Annex.
Notes: a. Average Annual Percentage of Total Adult Population, 1996–2005
b. Average Annual Percentage, 1996–2005
c. Per Hour Worked, Average Annual Percentage, 1996–2005
d. Average Annual Percentage Growth of Real GDP, 1996–2005
e. Average Annual Percent Increase of the GDP Deflator, 1996–2005
f. Government Net Lending as Percentage of GDP, Average Annual, 1996–2005

to be high. However, output and employment levels can still be high because labor markets can adjust to low productivity, even without pushing the economy into excessive deficits and inflation. The evidence, indeed, bears this out. One possible objection would be that labor-productivity growth is not that much lower than in the Fordist period, and it is questionable whether it warrants such a grandiose explanation as the shift from an industrial to a postindustrial age. Germany, as the paradigmatic case for the Christian-democratic social market, does also, at first glance, seem to confirm the Baumolitis thesis: high wages and generous social insurance have stultified service market expansion, resulting in high unemployment levels, which also act as a drag on output growth. The budget deficit is excessive, given the emphasis on monetary austerity and fiscal rectitude, but if one adjusts for the costs associated with German reunification, it is probably consistent with the fiscal burden on social insurance generated by high unemployment. However, labor-productivity growth is a lot lower than what one would expect from an economy based on export-oriented, high value–added manufacturing production. This could, of course, be interpreted as the social market economy performing even worse than anticipated. A less complacent reading, however, would be one that recognizes that such interpretation makes the situation more complicated than what the simple theory allows. One might, indeed, begin to discern alternative analyses of German stagnation. One would also remember that the issue of productivity, so central to the hypothesis, also gave grounds for scepticism in the US case.

However, it is the empirical evidence from Sweden, the paradigmatic case of a social-democratic welfare state, that delivers the devastating blow. With equally, if not more, highly decommodified labor markets and equally, if not more, generous social benefits than the Christian-democratic German case, Swedish social democracy empirically confounds the Baumolitis thesis. Its employment, unemployment, and output performance rates closely resemble those of the United States. They are slightly lower, but not by much. In addition, productivity growth is actually somewhat higher, and this is at full-capacity utilization (European Commission, 2003b). The explanation for this is not that difficult to find: in contrast to the Christian-democratic welfare state, which depends much more on traditional family networks and charities, a social-democratic welfare state has invested massively in the public service sector (for example, in child and elderly care, as well as in healthcare). It also has a highly developed labor market system of retraining and reactivation. This is, of course, recognized in much of the comparative literature (e.g., Esping-Andersen, 1990), which nevertheless predicts that this type of welfare state will face difficulties in containing inflation or in balancing budgets as it tries to maintain public service employment (Iversen and Wren, 1998); alternatively, high tax rates will choke growth. However, it is here that the Swedish case is the most confounding. Inflation rates are well below those of the United States (although not as low as the incredibly low 0.6 percent of Germany), and government net lending yields an annual average surplus of 1.3 percent of GDP. Indeed, these rates are probably sufficient to explain any gap in performance between the United States and Sweden with regard to employment and output growth.

The Scandinavian social democracies (one would find similar figures in Denmark, Norway, and Finland) are, of course, small countries, and one should be wary of offering them as models that can be copied by larger states or, certainly, by continentwide economies. In fact, they are prime examples of the niche strategies that we discuss below. Nevertheless, their cases clearly disprove the idea that Europe's stagnation can be reduced to the microeconomic supply-side bottlenecks of its comparatively decommodified labor markets.

The latter form of service employment expansion is often criticized by neoliberals as artificial; exacted at the price of economic efficiency, growth, and productivity; and increasingly counterproductive in an era of global competition. These arguments are made despite the fact that this form of welfare service employment growth has taken place in some of the most export-oriented economies of the OECD, some of which have experienced extremely high levels of import penetration.

European Self-Limitation

Above all, the Scandinavian cases suggest that welfare states committed to the development of a public service sector can still mobilize the positive externalities and economies from the welfare state of which the "variety of capitalism" literature speaks, including overcoming collective-action problems in labor-force training, in terms of the reduction of social overhead costs, and macroflexibility induced by social consensus (e.g., Gough, 1996; Katzenstein, 1985). Broader studies also confirm, just as in the case of employment, that there is little evidence of a correlation between a deregulated labor market and productivity (European Commission, 2001; Nickel, 1997). These conclusions are also consistent with firm-level studies showing that new information and communication technology is just as compatible with social market–style labor relations. There is evidence that such relationships provide the requisite functional flexibility—that is, "networking and skill to adjust volume to demand without productivity losses" (Amin, 1994: pp. 20–21)—via a highly skilled workforce in communication with management through codetermination practices (Boyer, 1995; Freyssenet, 1998; Standing, 2003).

When matters are seen in this light, the current EU strategy of copying the US experience is potentially counterproductive. While, as the US and British experiences show, it is possible to achieve sustained growth in this way, reforms in this direction are still greatly constrained by the residual power of unions, especially in the eurozone. Paradoxically, the inclusion of these unions as one of Issing's "social partners" was a precondition of the macroeconomic success of the German model (Hall and Franzese, 1998). Arguably, it is better for the eurozone to pursue a new economic trajectory embedded in these "negotiated involvement" institutions (Leborgne and Lipietz, 1988; Hollingsworth and Boyer, 1997).

However, such a development presupposes institutional and macroeconomic supports, and it is precisely in this context that the EMU has been self-limiting. Technology-driven productivity growth is stimulated by aggregate demand through so-called Kaldor-Verdoorn effects, and this seems especially important in social market economies with limited scope for cost cutting. Kaldor-Verdoorn effects result from stable and expansive demand. They ensure adequate investment levels and a stable environment for firms in which they become willing to experiment in the application, development, and diffusion of new technology through "learning by doing" (Boyer, 1995; Boyer and Petit, 1991).[5] This conjecture is consistent also with developments in the 1990s. As even the OECD argues, the sluggish growth in the eurozone, which is in such striking contrast to the growth in the United States and Britain, is not supply driven, but is rather caused by strong oscillations and, in the mid- to latter part of the decade, low levels of aggregate demand. Furthermore, the eurozone remains dependent on net exports and, most crucially, the US economy to pull it out of recessions (Organisation for Economic Co-operation and Development, 2003: pp. 22–25, 27; see also International Monetary Fund, 2004: pp. 48, 58).

To be sure, the OECD also points out that not only was actual GDP in the eurozone lower than that of the United States, but also potential GDP, a reflection of the increased productivity gap in the 1990s. The OECD's recommendation that the eurozone should seek to emulate the US deregulatory model is consistent with the Lisbon process. Yet, given the weak evidence of a correlation between such deregulation and productivity growth, it is more reasonable to infer that, in the context of technological change, the differences in aggregate demand growth are themselves the main cause of the productivity gap. Indeed, the evidence is more consistent with the Kaldor-Verdoorn thesis than with the eurosclerosis thesis. As the European Commission's (2003b) own studies find, the EU's lower growth in productivity is due to inadequate investment and innovation outside the non-ICT sectors of the economy ("inadequate diffusion"). Furthermore, two of the three EU states that (together with Ireland) achieved a higher level of productivity growth than did the United States at comparable utilization rates were among the most generous welfare states; namely, Sweden and Finland.

Although the OECD (2003) endorses the eurosclerosis thesis and the Lisbon agenda, its projections of the "predominant downside risks" illustrate quite clearly the European dilemma of our self-limitation thesis:

> Internal demand could be hit by stronger fiscal tightening than assumed in the projection, as countries that are currently subject to an "excessive deficit procedure" [Germany and France, representing 54 percent of eurozone GDP] under the rules of the Stability and Growth Pact may implement austerity packages. The simulations suggest that

a reduction of government consumption by 1 percent of GDP in Germany and France. . . . would reduce output by 1/2 percent from its baseline level in both the first and the second year. However, this does not take into account a possible impact of fiscal consolidation on confidence in financial markets and among households and businesses. (p. 27)

Leaving aside the demonstrably faulty conjecture that budget consolidation might generate a boost of demand through increased confidence of households,[6] this quote is quite illuminating. It is not only candid about the adverse effect that a strict adherence to the GSP would have on growth, it also points clearly to the trade-off between any attempt to boost aggregate demand and the terms upon which globalized financial markets grant credit in the eurozone. This stands in sharp contrast to the way in which credit structures have worked in the United States, where they have to a greater extent facilitated Kaldor-Verdoorn effects through the extension of public as well as private debt. This is the internal side of the dynamics discussed in the previous chapter with reference to Leonard Seabrooke's work.

Transitions from Fordism in the United States and Europe

The transition from the Fordist crisis in the 1970s to a sustainable "new economy" in the United States has entailed a temporal displacement of values in defunct Fordist enterprises to ventures in new sectors through debt, including the transfer of values to the United States from the rest of the world. In the monetarist global monetary system that was ushered in after the 1979 Volcker shock, this transition was only made possible through "the explosion of new financial instruments and markets coupled with the rise of highly sophisticated systems of financial coordination on a global scale" (Harvey, 1990: pp. 182–183). Centered around the dollar and Wall Street, as discussed in the previous chapter, this has resulted in a much tighter relationship between consumer, corporate, and government debt (pp. 194–195). Aided by these sophisticated structures, US military Keynesianism has sustained transnational capital accumulation, but it has done so in a way that systematically favors the United States, in relative terms, through the "exorbitant privileges." Hence, from the massive government deficits of the Reagan and Bush II administrations through the extraordinary expansion of private debt during the Clinton administration, capital accumulation has been sustained.

This is despite the debt crises in Latin America, the former Communist states, and East Asia. As pointed out in the previous chapter, the US-centered system has managed to turn these crises into a strengthening of institutions, since financial systems have been reconfigured to serve the Wall Street–dollar system.[7]

Flexible Liberalism in the United States

Consequently, the United States has embarked on a flexible, liberal form of the new, post-Fordist economy, facilitated through the progressive elimination of collective bargaining rights and the use of individualized contracts, incentives, threats, and flexible wages, all used to create an enterprise corporate culture. Flexible liberalism implies labor-market polarization, with a shrinking core workforce under enterprise contracts and a growing periphery of precariously employed workers. While the attendant wage cost reduction has a tendency to reduce aggregate demand, this is compensated for through an intensified consumption by the middle class and a reduction of turnover time of this consumption, particularly in the service sector. This consumption has typically been debt financed against the collateral of wealth accumulated in the increased values of real estate and the stock market. Of course, the financial sector is crucial to the expansion of consumption. It also plays an important role in the expansion of employment, both in the core labor market (financial services management, for example) and in the periphery (catering, cleaning, etc.) (e.g., Sassen, 1991). It is this system that the EU is trying to emulate through the SEM, EMU, and the Lisbon process. But this strategy is at odds with the fact that the EMU and the euro are assigned a totally different and subordinate position by global finance, in sharp contrast with the position assigned the United States and the dollar.[8]

Europe's subordinate role is evident not only in terms of the quantity of credit flows. Equally important are the disintegrative effects of the cumulative and integral dynamics of the foreign exchange markets and Euro-monetarism on the financial structures that have previously underpinned the growth models and national systems of innovation in the European social market economies. These effects have been admirably analyzed by John Grahl (2001; see also Story and Walter, 1997).

Europe's Halfway House

As is well-known, at least since the seminal work of Shonfield (1965), European social market economies have typically resolved the information asymmetry problems inherent in credit relationships through stable and long-term links between "housebank" bank creditors and corporate producers. These linkages produced dynamic systems of innovation, where bankers took a direct interest in industry and exercised credit power through their supervisory function. Hence, banks provided a mix of discipline and support that ensured the allocation of credit; such allocation took into account rational economic developments from a long-term perspective. These bank-corporate groupings also formed a coherent opposite number for the state and unions in bargaining over industrial policy, where social distributive and protection measures were exchanged for long-term, positive external effects of a highly trained and motivated workforce.

Even though blue-chip companies self-finance most of their investments through retained earnings (80 percent in the United States, 75 percent in France, and 65 percent in Germany), and international capital flows remain only a small part of total global investment activity,[9] Grahl (2001) argues that the "tail" of global finance "wags the dog." As a result, the European stakeholder systems are now progressively being colonized by the Anglo-Saxon shareholder system, where information asymmetry problems are resolved through creditors' continuous exit options, provided by the highly liquid range of money and capital markets. Despite their record of producing dynamic efficiency over time, the stakeholder systems suffer from the fact that each and every system is particular—indeed, each operates precisely through the particularities of its creditor-debtor relations. By contrast, the Anglo-Saxon system operates through the imposition of universal standards, and it can thus reproduce itself on a staggering scale.

The colonization works in the following way: Foreign exchange markets, with transactions on a truly massive, global scale (daily transactions were US$1.5 trillion in 1998), are creating a globally integrated and clearing payments system. Large banks draw short-term credit from any point of this payments system they please, and place any surplus wherever they please, in the financing of the imbalance of their positions. This means that any agent seeking short-term accommodation must, at the very least, match the terms of this global interbank market. According to Grahl (2001: pp. 30–32), this reconfigures the exchange equivalences, opportunity costs, and incentives of actors all the way down the chain of economic and social relationships in all parts of the world, or at least in the Euro-Atlantic economic space. This standardization of equivalences is fed into national credit structures through government bond issues, which increasingly have been directed toward global creditors and large banks, and whose yields are a key reference value for all credit instruments.[10]

To be sure, the stakeholder relationships are not immediately abandoned. Rather, the relationships are now being reassessed in a different context and by different criteria than those used in the past. In short, the foreign exchange and sovereign bond markets (that are global, liquid, and transparent) have reconfigured the opportunity costs of the stakeholder relations of corporate finance. In other words, they serve as the benchmark for other types of credit relationships (a benchmark that European monetary policy must, under current circumstances, maintain through "sound money policies" or risk a market-led deflation caused by a flight out of European bonds).

In the context of the new monetary policy regime, characterized by more unstable demand conditions, both European corporations and their bankers have begun to internalize the market terms set by these global markets. Especially in light of the shortening time-horizons that such conditions invite, Anglo-Saxon market-based creditors are offering reduced costs of capital to borrowers in ways that raise the return for lenders. This is because the scope and scale of the liquid markets allow for a diversification of risk, and the cumulative iterations of buying and selling of assets/liabilities reduce information costs. It should be noted that it is sufficient for *one* of the stakeholding parties to assess that this is the case for the relationship to break down, as these systems rely on the participation of all. In addition, once corporations begin to participate in these markets, the markets begin to exert disciplinary pressure through their demands for standardized accounting procedures and reporting conventions. They exert pressure on shareholder value and a maximization of profit within the "here and now." This has profound implications for enterprises: operating in a social market environment characterized by high overhead costs, including social overheads, they must attempt to extract the quid pro quo of social cohesion in exchange for long-term economic dynamism. According to Grahl (2001),

> To summarise the shareholder value agenda, one can look at matters from the point of view of the capital market itself—that is, in terms of the reallocation of capital resources. This market would see, on the one hand, over-capitalised enterprises situated in slow-growth sectors, perhaps with high earning streams but with relatively limited possibilities of accumulation. To the extent that they escape pressures from shareholders as principals, these "cash cows" may have acquired complex networks of

> insider coalition partners, representing stakeholder interests. To such a
> company, the shareholder value agenda is all too familiar. Pressures for
> productivity increases will involve downsizing, disposal of peripheral,
> under-performing divisions, stripping-out of cushioned managerial lay-
> ers and so forth. Financial reorganisation will include higher distribu-
> tion ratios, equity buybacks and increased gearing through the bond
> finance of assets that provide adequate collateral. In effect, sharehold-
> ers are saying: "there is no such thing as internal resources, everything
> is ours." Companies on which this programme has been imposed will
> provide higher returns on a possibly diminished equity base. This will
> correspond to higher risk for equity holders, but today's fund managers
> are confident that they can diversify those risks. (p. 39)

Naturally, in such a context the obsession with increasingly flexible
rules for hire and fire and wages becomes intelligible, as companies are
stripping out the infrastructure upon which the old productivity bargains
were based.

More broadly, the Lisbon and Cardiff agendas can be seen as institutional adjustments to the new conditions, driven by the imperatives of
the foreign exchange and equity markets. European elites seem intent
on reproducing Anglo-Saxon structures on a European scale in order to
create a viable platform upon which to compete with US capital in the
global economy. In other words, in contrast to the Etienne Davignon
concept of the late 1970s and early 1980s—when it was envisaged that
the nationally specific stakeholding relationships and industrial policy
structures of "national champions" would be replaced with a common
set of relations and policies of "European champions"—a highly liquid
European capital market should do the job (Holman and van der Pijl,
2003). In the pursuit of highest return through diversification strategies,
actors on such markets will reallocate resources to undercapitalized
starting-up projects in sunrise sectors. The problem is, however, that
current European restructuring most likely will stop at a halfway house,
where foreign exchange and bond markets have been integrated into
global circuits and thus have dismantled the old systems of innovation;
while stock markets, especially for venture capital (the equivalents of
NASDAQ), remain highly fragmented. Indeed, "mutual recognition"—
the method of negative integration upon which the SEM is based—has
not resulted in a breakdown of stock-market barriers. As a result, US-
style economies of scale do not obtain on European stock and venture
capital markets, and this holds back any emulation of the "American
model" of a new economy (Watson, 2001). While the Cardiff agenda
and the Financial Services Action Plan may result in positive policies

vis-à-vis some further European integration, there is, as Watson points out, a big difference between de jure and de facto integration. Furthermore, the EU is still a long way off from possessing the kind of retail banking sector that forms part of the US system; moreover, the formation of such a sector would entail a much deeper challenge to the social settlements. Current attempts to reform pensions are a step in that direction, but social conflicts, discussed in the next chapter, demonstrate that these are compounding legitimation-crisis tendencies. Moreover, these reforms are not eased by the absence of substantive economic growth. Hence, while FSAP includes elements of positive integration, these elements are far from engendering Europe's systems of economic innovation (Bieling, 2003).

As noted above, US economic dynamism in the 1990s was based on the mutually enforcing effects of that nation's integrated stock markets and expansive demand. We have already pointed out that this contradicts the norms (albeit increasingly contested) of the GSP and financial market confidence upon which the EMU rests. To counteract this, the eurozone would need, inter alia, to restructure public debt, ensure that it be denominated in euros (which would stabilize and reduce the interest charges on that debt), and establish a European financial center of sufficient scale to rival Wall Street in attracting savings and mobile capital (Boyer, 2000: p. 68). It is likely that the same would have to be done with regard to oil futures. This is not to mention the dramatic transition of retail banking required to generate interactive embeddedness. In other words, this analysis suggests a much more ambitious strategy for the eurozone than the EMU and Lisbon outlines, and one that would constitute a frontal challenge the Wall Street dollar regime. As we have shown, the EMU does not rise to this challenge.

Uneven Development and Problems of the Optimal Currency Area

In addition to the problem of adequate levels of growth, the EMU also raises questions about the spatial spread of growth within the territory of the currency area. Following Mundell, mainstream economics discusses this issue with reference to "asymmetric shocks" and "optimal currency areas." Asymmetric shocks occur when, all other things being equal, the demand for the products of one country goes up at the expense of another country's products (such as might be the case when consumer preferences change). If countries have different currencies, these changes in demand are regulated through appreciation and depreciation of currencies. However, in a monetary union, such changes might lead to more permanent drops in both output and employment in one country, and inflationary tendencies in the other. In addition, these imbalances can result from unsynchronized business cycles. Optimal currency areas are territories that have mechanisms to respond to such shocks and bring the market back to equilibrium. This could happen through one, or a combination, of the following: labor mobility over borders, flexibility of wages (which automatically increases wages in the country with an increase in demand for its products and decreases wages in the other country—this will create countervailing tendencies of demand), or integrated financial markets (which will spread the wealth effects if asset holders reside over the entire territory encompassed by the currency union) (De Grauwe, 2003).

Not surprisingly, the architects of the monetary union justify the pursuit of the Lisbon agenda of deregulation with reference to the concept of an optimal currency area. Yet, there are good reasons to be pessimistic. Capital markets remain highly segmented and are likely to be in a hub-and-spoke relationship to one another through London, the non-eurozone financial center of Europe. Wage flexibility, on the other hand, is caught between the assault on union rights implied by Lisbon and the residual power that trade unions retain. It has been argued that corporatist wage coordination remains the only mechanism of adjustment left in the hands of member states after the EMU (Crouch, 2000). This is true; and in certain territories, privileged in the European division of labor, these relationships might persist.[11] However, it is exactly these structures that the shareholder value agenda tends to undermine. Because outright dismantling of union power in an Anglo-Saxon direction is unlikely in the foreseeable future, it is probable that wage rigidities will actually increase.[12] Furthermore, there are strong linguistic, cultural, as well as institutional barriers to large-scale labor mobility within the eurozone (for instance, the transferability of pensions is an uncertain matter).

Despite these considerations, the European Commission (1990) argues that a high degree of intra-industry trade nevertheless makes the eurozone conform to optimal currency area criteria. This conformity would tend to produce an even development of productivity growth and absence of asymmetrical shocks, because changes in supply and demand tend to affect countries in a similar way. This argument has been challenged on the basis of polarization thesis, first associated with Gunnar Myrdal and the original dependency theorists at the Economic Commission for Latin America: single market dynamics lead not to diffusion, but rather to concentration of economic growth. In a single market system, it becomes possible to locate production closer to final markets and to concentrate production to optimize economies of scale. This leads to an uneven spread of productivity growth, which manifests itself as an asymmetric shock. Krugman (1991, cited in De Grauwe, 2003: p. 25; see also Dicken, 1998) expands the analysis by including proximity to R&D networks, skilled workers, and intermediary producers in just-in-time production. Notwithstanding these findings, De Grauwe upholds the views of the commission because the centralization/peripheralization dynamic most likely transgresses state borders (De Grauwe, 2003: p. 27).

Even if the latter is the case, this is not sufficient to dismiss the likelihood of an increase in the variation of growth and productivity for the EMU. First, it cannot be assumed that these variations will *always* transgress borders nor that they will do so symmetrically. Second, nation-states themselves have rarely been optimal currency areas (this includes the United States, as Mundell himself argued). To sustain economic balance, it has therefore been commonplace to develop "fiscal federalism" and transfer-payments systems that redistribute some of the economic surplus to the periphery. Seen from this perspective, the fact that fiscal policy and systems continue to be nationally fragmented is a pressing problem (MacKay, 1995). The most effective regional stabilizers are usually automatic stabilizers out of national budgets, but these do, of course, only have a national scope. In response to this problem, in 1977 the MacDougall Report recommended a common EU budget of 5 to 7 percent of GDP, which was within the framework of the more modest aims of the Common Market, without EMU and without anticipating eastern enlargement. By contrast, EU's common budget is 1.2 percent of GDP, with an increased demand on its regional policy resources after successive eastern enlargements.

What is more, there are good reasons to suspect that the defensive and market-conforming structural transformation that competitive austerity generates, now further enhanced through the National Action Plans of the Lisbon agenda, also has adverse effects on macroeconomic stabilization policy. This is because of the negative impact on "automatic stabilizers" of tax and benefit systems "reforms" (Mabbett and Schelkle, 2005). In a generally stagnant economic environment, where countries have surrendered stabilization instruments, these policies produce political fragmentation and conflict, as exemplified by the 2003–2004 crisis of the GSP (discussed in Chapter 2).

Unless the Union budget increases substantially and a European fiscal policy is developed, the realities of uneven development will sooner or later threaten the stability of the SEM and the EMU. There is indeed a disintegrative or "reverse spillover" effect in the eurozone: as the previous chapter demonstrated, the inability to respond to uneven development through depreciation tends to lead to demands for fiscal expansion; constraints on national fiscal policy, however attenuated (but a matter only of pact, rather than treaty), in turn produce renewed drives toward "economic patriotism" in the sphere of trade policy.

However, if uneven development exacerbates economic problems, it is also in the nature of competitive austerity to make it more difficult to generate a consensus and collective action to address these problems. Different states, regions, and social groups—often transgressing class divides, pitting some workers against others—have different capacities to engage in the competitive austerity game. The end result of such collective action problems might, paradoxically, be the consolidation, rather than the undermining, of neoliberalism—this consolidation fed by a cycle of defections, by the undermining of solidarity, and by lack of trust in collective solutions (Offe, 1997). In some locales, distributive coalitions of capitalists and wage earners may generate rather broad-based consent around neoliberal restructuring because of a fortuitous position in the regional division of labor. In such locales, export-oriented, high value–added specialization may help sustain growth models based on high rates of productivity growth and positive-sum distribution of surplus in an intensive accumulation process, despite the general state of austerity in the eurozone as a whole.

The conclusions reached by research in the field of economic geography are immensely helpful in illuminating these tendencies. They point to the continued salience of agglomeration economies in the European economy, despite the reduction of information bottlenecks and transportation and transaction costs, inter alia, proximity to customers and intermediary producers, an appropriately skilled workforce, and research and development infrastructure continue to be crucial for high value–added production. Integration of the European economy since the 1980s has resulted in a perhaps sharpened polarization of core-periphery relations across and within member states (Dicken, 1998; Smith, Rainnie, and Dunford, 2001; Dunford, 2005). The research points to the clustering of high value–added production in Europe's "blue banana," with one end in Tuscany and Emilia-Romagna, reaching up via the confluences of the Rhine and environs to southeastern England. (In addition, there is a clustering of core-activities in other prosperous centers around such cities as Hamburg and Paris.) These are the centers of Europe's research-intensive biomedical industry, capital-intensive and process-innovative traditional industries, and the business service industry. The diffusion of economic activity to the periphery, insofar as it happens at all, is restricted to low value–added commodities, where labor costs are of crucial significance.

The presence of these clusters does not, however, represent a straightforward continuation of the Keynesian and Fordist configuration, with a stark demarcation between welfare states in the north, capable of generating and distributing economic rents, and a periphery that is unable to extract such "relative gains" from the international/European division of labor. First, high value–added commodities are nowadays produced with higher levels of capital intensity, a development that excludes a large part of the labor force from the circles of privilege. Second, the clustering of high value–added commodities does not coincide with the politico-administrative borders of states in charge of redistribution through tax-financed transfer payments. This has resulted in increased inequalities and growing pressure on welfare safety nets.

Competitive Austerity and the Fragmentation of Interests

The fact of uneven development under conditions of competitive austerity is a crucial factor in producing divisions over the extent and content of the EU's social dimension and attendant "nondecisions," ensuring that "negative" market integration is not followed up with countervailing supranational "positive integration" (e.g., Scharpf, 1996). For example, the Netherlands, a state with entrenched "social capitalist" institutions and ethos, managed in the 1990s to boost employment growth and achieve fiscal balance while engaging in a limited form of welfare-state retrenchment. The Polder model was based on concession bargaining and wage segmentation, the creation of a two-tier social insurance system, and adoption of active labor-market policy through corporatist consensus (Visser and Hemerijck, 1997). This was done while the Netherlands adopted a highly orthodox stance on the SEM, EMU, and the GSP. But this was a niche strategy that could not have been sustained without fortuitous circumstances. These include: Dutch access to independent energy in the form of North Sea gas, the Netherlands' position as a European transport hub, and its location in relation to Germany, which allowed the former to just undercut German social costs in wage competition (Becker, 2000; Ryner, 2002: chapter 2). These conditions mitigated the contradictions between flexible liberal changes and the social market discourses and institutions of legitimacy. Similar conditions obtained in Denmark, which was even more successful in mediating flexible liberalism with welfare-state protection (e.g., Torfing, 1999; Goul Andersen, 2003).

The critical importance of niche strategies and the differential conditions of growth models is underlined by the history of Germany. From the 1970s to recent times, the German Bundesbank was, via the EMS, the linchpin ensuring that Europe was integrated into the system of US minimal hegemony, while having one of the most advanced welfare states on the continent. This was possible exactly because of the particular configuration of its export sector. Germany's monetary policy stance and participation in the EMS formed an important part of that nation's welfare-state bargain after the oil crises and the collapse of the Bretton Woods system. As described in the previous chapter, a noninflationary "hard mark" policy reduced energy costs for German export-oriented manufacturing and facilitated the redistribution, or "rents," to organized labor engaged in "responsible" tripartite bargaining. The costs of imported consumption goods were also reduced. The ERM served the function of containing competitive devaluations inside the EC (Lankowski, 1982; Riemer, 1982). The bargain was conditional on favorable terms of trade (denominated in dollars) and on the possibility of using wage bargaining for welfare-state redistribution.

But recent events have demonstrated the dependency implied in these niche strategies, also, for the largest European economy. The costs associated with German reunification reduced terms of trade and increased capital intensity, and the adoption of outsourcing strategies by German business has undermined these conditions. In an ironic twist, France's move toward a more austerity-based competitive disinflation has also deprived Germany of an important source of demand-pull for its exports (Deubner, Rehfeld, and Schlupp, 1992). In other words, in the German case, the contradictions between neoliberal restructuring and the social market are mounting (Ryner, 2003). The German case also brings home the point that competitive austerity is a zero-sum game that cannot be part of a general solution to the problem of relaunching the dynamism of eurocapitalism (Boyer, 1990).

Uneven development also contributes to the fragmentation of interests in the periphery. In the short run, at least, some constituencies can be mobilized for the current configurations of the SEM and the EMU. When markets are opened to social systems with high social wages, economies generated from wage competition might serve to improve social standards, especially when bolstered by the Common Agricultural Policy and regional policy (Ross, 1995). This seems to have been the experience of the "core in the periphery" regions in southern Europe, at least. In the 1990s, Spanish GDP per capita increased from 72.5 to 82.5 percent of the EU-15 average, with Madrid, the Basque Country, and Navarra now having a per capita income above this average. (Greek and Portuguese GDP per capita, as a percentage of the EU-15 average, increased, respectively, from 58.3 to 66.8 percent and from 59.2 to 76.1 percent [European Commission, 2003c, cited in Holman, 2004b: p. 220]). In addition, Holman argues that Spanish business has undergone a restructuring that has made it more competitive and capable of pursuing export-oriented strategies. As a result of this, although unemployment remains high, it has come down significantly from the astronomical rates of over 20 percent in the early 1990s (p. 220).

It should be pointed out, though, that these aggregate figures still mask significant regional inequalities within Spain, Portugal, and Greece and that even aggregate unemployment rates remain around 10 percent. In any case, Holman also argues that, in the absence of a domestic bourgeoisie, a much stronger conditionality in terms of macroeconomic austerity and an absence of comparable regional policy means that a replication of the southern European "success" is unlikely in the new member-states of Central and Eastern Europe (the CEECs) (pp. 221–229). Here, the beneficial effects of foreign direct investment and "Ricardian" economies of comparative advantage are likely to be limited to subcontracting operations at the borders to western Europe and to second-tier business services in the capital regions. The division of labor is assigning low productivity, low value–added activities to the CEECs, with little prospect of an upgrade (Petrakos, Maier, and Gorzelak, 2000).

The Conjuncture of 2005–2007: Recovery in Perspective

Beginning in the latter part of 2005, the eurozone began to experience a cyclical recovery. Although not large at all by historical standards, and significant largely in the context of the abysmal record over the prior five-year period, it resulted in an overall growth rate in the eurozone of 2 percent for the first two quarters of 2006. Between November 2005 and November 2006, unemployment fell from 9.3 to 8.0 percent in Germany and from 9.6 to 8.6 percent in France (OECD, 2007). The recovery was seen as a vindication of ECB policies and, more generally, the Lisbon process, and it served as a call to action for further reforms. Joaquin Almunia, the EU monetary affairs commissioner, stated, "We are starting a recovery and we have a list of structural reforms that are paying off" (Parker and Atkins, 2006: p. 3). Ann Mettler, director of the Lisbon Council, suggested, "It is easier for the Commission to promote reforms at the moment because after years of gloomy reports we can see higher economic growth and lower unemployment in Europe, mainly in countries that did make such reforms (*EUobserver,* 2006b: p. 1). In its *Economic Survey of the Euro Area 2007,* the OECD called for governments to ease employment protection legislation, boost wage flexibility, and make greater efforts toward fiscal consolidation (OECD, 2007: pp. 5–8). However, the nature of the recovery, modest and highly uneven by historical standards, by no means vindicates the strategy of monetarism and structural labor reform. Rather, by further illustrating the depth of the problems of uneven development and self-limitation, it provides further evidence of a coming crisis of a Union in which monetary policy is centralized while all other important policy instruments remain in the hands of the member states.

The recovery was largely centered on Germany, and apart from the temporary boost of the 2006 World Cup soccer tournament, it has been based heavily on export-led growth, coupled with structural reform of German labor markets. The share of wages in GDP declined significantly between 1991 and 2005 (European Commission, 2006c), a trend encouraged by widespread outsourcing in central and eastern Europe, as well as extremely high levels of German foreign direct investment, much of which has flowed to the United States (see Chapter 4). The achievement of a relatively modest growth rate—2.5 percent—yielded record corporate profits as well as exports. While not very impressive by historical standards, this return of Germany's classical export-driven stance, combined with neoliberal deepening, is highly significant. By 2003, Germany had overtaken the United States as the world's largest exporter in *total* terms, not merely as a percentage of GDP. In 2004, German companies exported approximately $1 trillion of products, equal to the combined exports of Britain, the Netherlands, and France. Germany's trade surplus was six times as large as that of China. Moreover, the sales of Germany's foreign affiliates exceeded German exports (Benoit and Milne, 2006: p. 11). Within the eurozone, Germany registered substantial trade surpluses with virtually all of its trading partners, as the policy of austerity represented an effective competitive devaluation.

To be sure, given the size of the German economy, its own growth rates did translate into a more general recovery throughout the eurozone. However, the results of this recovery have been uneven and deeply problematic and destabilizing for other members. Germany has imposed massive fiscal and social pressures on other member states. As Paul de Grauwe has written, "It is no exaggeration to state that Germany has followed a policy of 'beggar thy neighbour' reminiscent of similar policies in the 1930s. As a result, it has exported its problems to the other eurozone countries, which are likely to retaliate" (De Grauwe, 2006b: p. 13). In the context of the EMU straitjacket, retaliation occurs through further "competitive austerity" in the form of wage cuts, further depressing demand and employment, and competitive "fiscal dumping" (Parker, 2006: p. 2). The limitations of this essentially mercantilist strategy have led to only very weak recoveries in France and Italy. As a result of the renegotiation of the GSP, Italy has been able to avoid reductions in public debt, thereby prolonging its own fiscal crisis even as its industries become less competitive. Not surprisingly, France has become increasingly vocal in its attacks on the monetarist policies of the ECB. After many years of austerity, increasing labor militancy—most notably in Germany—has led ECB to reduce the scope of the recovery by raising interest rates. Yet, it is doubtful that in Germany's developing two-tier labor market, characterized by a growing stratum of unprotected and precarious workers, wage increases can provide the basis for sustained, domestic, demand-led growth. With its strong export emphasis, the German economy remains dependent on the United States as a locomotive and highly vulnerable to global macroeconomic turbulence. However, as we discuss in Chapter 5, the US economy itself is under strain; the locomotive may be running out of steam.

Notes

1. Between 1961 and 1973, average annual labor productivity in what is now the eurozone was 4.9 percent. Total factor productivity was 3.3 percent (European Commission, 2006a: p. 196).

2. Between 1961 and 1973, US average annual labor productivity growth was 2.4 percent. Total factor productivity was 2.0 percent (European Commission, 2006a: p. 215).

3. For a useful overview of the Lisbon, Cardiff, and Luxembourg processes of labor-market reform, see Organisation for Economic Co-operation and Development (2002: pp. 111–142).

4. On the contrast between ECB theory and practice, see CEPR (2002), cited in Talani (2005). For a critique of the neoclassical framework on which the monetarist doctrine of the EMU rests, which emphasizes the importance of

dynamic efficiency, technological change, and institutional complementarity of norms of production and consumption rather than mid-term general equilibrium, see Boyer (2000).

5. The thesis is given empirical substantiation for the 1970s and 1980s in the OECD area, which points to a strong cumulative, causal relationship between productivity growth and effective demand (pp. 50–55 and 61–62). "Solow's productivity paradox" in the 1980s—the coexistence of rapid technological change and stagnant productivity growth—is strongly related to sluggish and uneven growth in aggregate demand, while comparative growth figures in the 1970s, despite limited technological change, are related to expansive (if inflationary) demand in that period. Boyer's interpretation that the disappointing developments are due to the limited diffusion of new technology from a restricted cluster of vanguard sectors is verified by the Organisation for Economic Co-operation and Development (1988).

6. The budgetary consolidation of 2004, such as the radical reforms in the German social insurance system, resulted in a sharp increase of precautionary savings, which totally preempted any consumer-led growth (Munchau, 2004).

7. As Arrighi (1994) observes, historically these are the kinds of privileges that declining hegemons enjoy in financial markets, which temporally displace hegemonic decline. In the end, however, the massive debts that the hegemon accumulates will result in a transfer of value to contenders (as in the case of post–World War I US-British relations). In the early 1990s, much was made of Japanese corporate takeovers in the United States. However, as Arrighi observes, the intricacies of US corporate structures ensured that the Japanese investor failed to gain adequate control and return on their investments, and it may be that the deals, in the end, benefited the United States more than Japan. Certainly, developments since the Asian crisis suggest that this is the case.

8. On this, see Heiner Ganssmann's (2004: p. 13) critique of the prescriptions underlying the Agenda 2010 reforms in Germany. Ganssmann invokes Solow's Nobel Laureate lecture (quoted in the introduction to this chapter), which suggests that the eurosclerosis thesis rests on "the naïve belief that unemployment must be a defect of the labor market, as if the hole in a flat tyre must always be on the bottom, because that is where the tyre is flat" (Solow, 2000: p. 7). Ganssmann goes on to show that there is no correlation between the deterioration of Germany's economic performance and German wage increases. Indeed, the stagnation of the 1990s coincided with a marked increase of the profit over wage share of national income. Rather, the problem is due, in part, to financing the cost of reunification via the social insurance system and exchange rate movements; but the most important reason is the "catastrophic" fall of net investment from 22 percent of national income in the 1970s to 3.5 percent, despite higher rates of profits. This is not due to a lack of investment capital, but rather due to capital outflows. Between 1998 and 2001, foreign direct investment volumes increased from 302 billion euros to 628 billion euros (total net domestic investment was 372 billion euros). Also, portfolio outward investments rose until the 2001 crash. The reason for this is that, despite increased rates of profit, German capital perceived prospects of even higher rates of profit abroad and was sucked into "a maelstrom of high US profits, speculation and greed." With regard to the latter point, Ganssmann takes too much at face value the view of German investors themselves. As argued in the

previous chapter with reference to the work of Duménil and Lévy (2003), the overall returns on foreign investments in the United States tend to be comparatively low. Instead, the United States draws a premium as the haven of capitalism and its seignorage status.

9. This has been the cornerstone of evidence invoked by those who assert the continued salience of national economic autonomy (e.g., Hirst and Thompson, 1996).

10. The euro has greatly facilitated the expansion of a European bond market, such that the euro has now outpaced the dollar as the largest currency in international bond markets. In some modest respects, this represents a challenge to the role of the dollar. Yet, it also indicates the extent to which European companies are "abandoning their traditional reliance on bank loans and turning to capital markets" (Oakley and Tett, 2007: p. 13).

11. Here one should also note sources of instability. The competitive corporatist accords in places like the Netherlands in the 1990s took place against the backdrop of high unemployment. When adjustments then take place through corporatist concertation, and unemployment is reduced, it becomes difficult to sustain the arrangements in a competitive austerity framework, as unions, representing their members, seek to recover previous gaps between wage and productivity growth (Ryner and Schulten, 2003).

12. On the "bell-shaped" nature of wage rigidity (where flexibility is facilitated either by highly decentralized or highly centralized wage bargaining), the standard reference is Calmfors and Driffil (1988).

4

The Limits of Euro-Legitimacy

We were very clear in the talks [with the IG Metall union]. We said, "We have Poland. We have Hungary. We have the Czech Republic."
—Jürgen Schrempp, Chief Executive, DaimlerChrysler AG (quoted in Boudette, 2004: p. 1)

The big "peoples parties" are withering in all countries . . . [they] circle each other like boxers in the late rounds of a prize fight.
—Christopher Caldwell (2005: p. 11)

In Chapter 2, we explored Europe's subordination to the structural power of the United States through the dollar and transnational finance. Chapter 3 discussed the implications of this for the European economy. EMU has spearheaded Europe's second project of integration, but it has not resulted in stable growth and full employment, as the architects of the monetary union (and SEM) anticipated. Rather, it has resulted in competitive austerity; stagnant productivity, output, and employment growth; high unemployment; and uneven development. This chapter focuses on the implications of neoliberalism for sociopolitical representation and legitimacy. This inevitably entails a focus on the coming crisis of the welfare state, given the central importance assigned to social citizenship in Europe.

At the outset, we hasten to acknowledge that stagnant and polarizing economic conditions do not automatically generate sociopolitical crises. The economic reductionist assumption to that effect, which has marred liberal as well as socialist analyses too often, assumes away the need to explain the complex relationship between the socioeconomic and the sociopolitical. Influential analysts have argued that European welfare systems can weather the storm of economic stagnation within the framework of the EMU. Indeed, it has been argued that the EMU is actually *strengthening* the welfare state. The most articulate advocates of this view are Anton Hemerijck (2002) and Martin Rhodes (2002).

Following a brief introduction to the nature of the post–World War II variants of the European social model or—perhaps more to the point—models, this chapter will consider and refute the theses of Rhodes and Hemerijck. Contrary to their analyses, we argue that the Euro-centered macroeconomic regime, as outlined in the previous chapters, is singularly ill-suited for reconfiguring European welfare capitalism. At the same time, the EMU has been presented in the mass-political arena as compatible with the European social model(s), and the ground has not been prepared for a successful adaptation of an Anglo-US model. Indeed, drawing on the analysis of the previous two chapters, since the Anglo-US model depends on the "exorbitant privileges" linked to the global supremacy of the dollar, we argue that this adaptation is, at the very least, deeply problematic given the subordinate position of the euro. The final part of this chapter explains how the pressures on European welfare capitalism translate into a political crisis of legitimacy and representation. Particular, but by no means exclusive, attention is here given to the two largest states at the very core of the eurozone—France and Germany.

The European Social Model(s)

Discussions of European reform that emphasize the importance of increasing market conformity and flexibility are problematic not only from a narrow economic point of view, as indicated in Chapter 3. They are problematic also because they rest on an implicit and voluntarist assumption that social policy is a "generosity"—a sort of charity and indulgence that can be withdrawn in times of necessity. This view is contradicted by virtually all social scientific research into the nature and significance of the welfare state in European political economy and, more broadly, in the political economy of the advanced capitalist OECD world. Since the seminal work by Harold Wilensky (1975), we have known that the welfare state has become an essential functional component of industrial society. The observed correlations between increased GDP per capita and social expenditure (irrespective of the political ideology of the dominant political parties) is not only explained by the capacity to spend; much more significantly, it is explained by the *need* of these societies to make such expenditure to maintain social order. When societies industrialize, communal support structures of traditional, agrarian, Gemeinschaft society, and the extended family are broken down. As the logic of the industrial capitalist marketplace begins to take hold, these structures are not spontaneously replaced by other institutions capable of performing social caring and reproductive functions necessary for a society where there is an increasing lack of synchronicity between material needs associated with the human lifecycle and the capacity to engage in productive work (leading to the problems of providing childcare, education, healthcare, and care of the elderly). Furthermore, new risks emerge (industrial accidents, urban sanitary problems, and, indeed, unemployment). Here, the complex, made up of publicly financed social services, insurance, protective legislation, as well collective bargaining regimes—the constituent components of the welfare state—becomes an important stabilizer, since it satisfies these new social needs. In the wake of further attenuation of community networks and the transformation of family life in the current juncture (also in response to the increased aspirations of women to take full part in civil societal and working life), there is no reason to suppose that the demands that require a welfare state have relented. The degree to which they will be met and on what terms, is, of course, another story (Esping-Andersen, 1999).

Apart from this "mechanical" function, the welfare state has also been essential for sociopolitical legitimacy. This is especially the case in Europe. It is no exaggeration to say that here the welfare state played a crucial role in reconciling capitalist markets with political democracy in the second half of the twentieth century. To understand the significance of the welfare state for legitimacy, it is essential to appreciate the centrality of *social citizenship* and its attendant rights, and their relationship to civic and political rights. According to a seminal argument by T. H. Marshall (1950), the vast mass of the population, which is materially dependent on waged work, can only exercise civil and political rights through social rights. In other words, it is only when risks of destitution and insecurity associated with industrial capitalist society are eliminated, or at least substantially mitigated, through the social rights provided by the welfare state that the broad mass of the population can fully obtain the status required to effectively exercise civic and political citizenship. This normative principle underpins, with variations, the various social accords between, inter alia, classes, confessional, regional, and linguistic groups in European states and societies (Esping-Andersen, 1990).

A significant part of the reason why the social protection of the welfare state is such an important legitimation constraint in the eurozone is to be found in the particular historical legacy of capitalist development and modernization in continental Europe. In contrast to the British case, industrialization did not occur until the latter part of the nineteenth century, at a time when the dominant production technologies and sectors (the increased application of formal science in mechanical and chemical engineering) engendered a logic based on economies of scale (Gerschenkron, 1962). This led to collective action and state intervention (as opposed to laissez-faire) in neomercantilist catch-up strategies. Hence, when economic and industrial elites faced the protests and revolutionary agitation of the labor movements of the late nineteenth and early twentieth centuries, it was not a remote idea that social integration of workers should be secured through state intervention and consensus formation inspired by corporative traditions. Christian norms of charity and a concern for the less fortunate provided an ethical orientation in this context, as did the incentive to mobilize the working class for the cause of national unity (which, in some cases, as in France, entailed a consolidation of working-class identity with the republican revolutionary legacy). The Bismarck reforms in Germany in the 1880s were paradigmatic (e.g., Briggs, 1969: pp. 21–25). At the same time, given the rapid nature of transformation, the historical memory of the labor movements of continental Europe, which included craft traditions and the estates, facilitated a disposition toward corporatism. This provided the basis of a quid pro quo for cooperation in industrial restructuring and productivity growth strategies in exchange for social protection, which continues to provide a normative orientation in European civil societies to this day. In the words of Hemerijck (2002: p. 1), "At the cognitive level, the European social model is based on the *recognition that social justice can contribute to economic efficiency and progress*" (italics in original).

On the downside, this socioeconomic structure, based on a high degree of concentration of control and economies of scale, is vulnerable in an environment of uncertain market developments. Above all, the turbulence characteristic of the interwar financial system and the Great Depression demonstrated this. In addition, in many countries, elites opted for repressive solutions to the problems of the 1920s and 1930s. It was only after World War II—paradoxically, under US leadership, institutions, and such programs and organizations as the Marshall Plan, the Organization for European Cooperation (OEEC), and the Bretton Woods system—that a variant of this state-interventionist and state-corporatist form of capitalism was firmly rendered compatible with liberal democracy, labor inclusion, and the welfare state. On the basis of different Fordist formulas, then, Europe experienced "the Thirty Glorious Years" *(les trentes glorieuses)* of European social capitalism under integral US Keynesian hegemony.

Welfare-State Variations

Following the influential work of Esping-Andersen (1990), it is possible to identify three generally recognized ideal types of welfare-state accords and regimes in Europe after World War II. Arguably, there is also a fourth one, of a more recent origin, in the southern European states that underwent a democratic transition in the 1970s (Ferrera, 1996; Arts and Gelissen, 2002). The liberal welfare state reflects a sociopolitical accord where the bourgeoisie remains dominant not only in economic life, but also in political life; and where wage earners' demands are integrated as concessions. This captures the essentials of the situation in the United Kingdom, Ireland, and, indeed, the United States. Some universalist social programs were developed (e.g., the National Health Service), but these provide services only at minimum standards, considering budget constraints and limited prospects of tax increases. Means-tested benefits play a central role in this type of system, and the well-to-do, in search of better quality, continue to have strong incentives to seek alternative, private arrangements. Economic measures intended to combat unemployment are pursued, but with due regard to the policy conflict between this objective and that of price stability (as expressed by the Phillips curve). The collective bargaining regime remains centered on the company level and is poorly integrated with other aspects of the welfare state. This is a "residual" welfare state, where market logic remains dominant even in the provision of welfare. The welfare state is construed as a safety net for those who are unable to fend for themselves adequately in the marketplace.

By contrast, the social-democratic welfare state provides an unconditional commitment to full employment and develops a universalism in social policy, funded by high taxes, appealing to the entire population by providing a normal standard of living. Finally, highly organized, centralized, and strong trade unions provide leadership in the formulation of economic policy, articulating it together with a coherent "solidaristic wage policy." This model reflects the social accords of the Scandinavian countries, the only countries in Europe where Second International social democracy became hegemonic in the political sphere. In Scandinavia, economic power remains with a highly centralized capitalist class, and the political economy is regulated through accommodation and negotiation between the two power centers—the capitalists and the unions.

However, from the point of view of the eurozone, the Christian-democratic welfare state is by far the most prominent model. It characterizes the essential welfare-state arrangements of most EMU members, and certainly those of the core area of the eurozone. This welfare state is, in many respects, functionally equivalent to the social-democratic state in terms of social expenditure and the generous replacement rates it offers in social-insurance schemes (van Kersbergen, 1995). It also comes close to the social-democratic regimes in the status accorded to trade unions both in wage determination and as a social partner in corporatist deliberation on economic policy. Typically, collective bargaining agreements cover the entire labor market; and labor law grants codetermination rights in the workplace. In other words, the degree of social protection from the vagaries of the market is substantial. But the qualitative nature of Christian-democratic social programs differs from the social-democratic variants quite substantially. Rather than providing universalism and redistribution, the Christian-democratic welfare state is geared toward income replacement and maintenance of *existing* social status groups, who pay into, and accrue benefits from, group-specific funds. This type of welfare state not only lacks a universalist framework, but also does not share the social-democratic commitments to develop welfare-state services, such as childcare. This reticence reflects a commitment toward the reproduction of traditional civil-societal institutions, including a familialist commitment to the traditional family: a male breadwinner and a female household caretaker. Finally, full employment is not an unconditional goal in this type of welfare state; price stability is seen as an equally—if not more—important economic policy goal, as in the liberal welfare states. This is a welfare-state regime where decommodification is combined with a fundamental commitment to private property. In contrast to the social-democratic welfare states' conditional acceptance of private property, which reserves the option of challenging private property if social goals are not met, the Christian-democratic welfare state *redeems* capitalism by engendering it with social responsibility and reflexivity. This welfare-state variety expresses an accord where the sociopolitical power of both organized business and labor is substantial, but where neither is sufficient to obtain political hegemony. Christian democracy has, instead, become hegemonic here because of its exceptional capacity to assume the role of a *mediator.* Christian democracy and social capitalism have thus demonstrated remarkable capacities to mediate between these capitalist and societal interests, as well as between those of confessional and/or linguistic groups. Indeed, Christian democracy can be defined quintessentially through this "politics of mediation." That is, "a religiously inspired, ideologically condensed and politically practiced conviction that conflicts of interests can and must be reconciled politically in order to restore the natural and organic harmony of society" (van Kersbergen, 1995: p. 2).

This particular framework for managing cleavages has enabled Christian democracy to accumulate political power resources and to inhibit the hegemonic capacities of liberalism and socialism. Christian democracy has enjoyed some remarkable success in the postwar period. This includes the reconciliation of class conflict in Germany (and Austria) within a liberal, democratic framework—a conflict that had destroyed the Weimar Republic and paved the way for the Nazi regime. While social consensus was less explicit and more ambivalent in Italy and France, the Italian Christian Democrats and the French Gaullists nevertheless achieved a remarkable degree of social integration and modernization in societies where fundamental social conflict between right-wing and left-wing extremes had previously been combined with economic stagnation. The Dutch and Belgian postwar experiences built on social compromises begun in the interwar period, which not only mediated between the left and right, but also between Catholics, Protestants, and atheists, and between Dutch and French speakers. The welfare state was the central institutional expression and mechanism of this social peace formula (van Kersbergen, 1995).

A few words should also be said about the welfare states in the Mediterranean periphery of the eurozone (Spain, Portugal, Greece). In many respects, in qualitative terms these resemble those of the Christian-democratic ideal type, insofar as social-insurance schemes are fragmented rather than universal and insofar as familialism and religion feature as underlying norms of welfare-state institutions. However, these welfare states do not have the same minimum standards of their northern Christian-democratic neighbors, and the social expenditure per GDP is much lower (arguably reflecting a lower degree of economic development). In addition, these states tend to have universal programs for healthcare.

A Crisis of Social Citizenship?

The European welfare states developed during the Fordist golden age against the backdrop of economic conditions that, in many fundamental respects, were the opposite of those outlined in the previous chapter. In contrast to the sluggishness of present-day growth rates, this was a period of rapid output and productivity growth. Also, in contrast to the present period of European mass unemployment, during this period economies were operating at, or close to, full employment. Furthermore, there existed a mutually supportive relationship between the dynamics of the social market economy and the welfare state. The social market economy provided the resources that enabled welfare-state expansion; and, according to the Fordist formula, the welfare state helped ensure stable and expanding demand for mass-produced products through wage settlements, public investments in welfare services, and the automatic stabilizers of the social-insurance programs. This underpinned the trust between the social partners required for acceptance of economic rationalization in exchange for protection against social risk.

It is logical to suppose, then, that low growth rates and high unemployment accounted for in the previous chapter are going to have debilitating impacts on the European welfare states. If nothing else, low growth rates and high unemployment reduce receipts from taxes and payroll surcharges at the same time as the claims on social insurance increase, generating fiscal imbalances. This is especially the case in the Christian-democratic welfare states, where there is a direct relationship between employment and the fiscal balance of social insurance as a result of the vocation-specific nature of program benefits and revenues. It should be underlined here that what was originally seen as a solution has, in the long run, exacerbated the problems. In the 1980s, a policy of work reduction and early retirement in exchange for labor acquiescence to technological change, even if it meant labor shedding, was seen as a solution that combined economic dynamism, productivity, and competitiveness with the welfare state. This policy is increasingly seen as a dead-end strategy. The reason is that ever-fewer workers and employers have to pay ever-higher payroll surcharges to sustain the income replacement claims of unemployed and retired workers, thus increasing nonwage labor costs. This, it is argued, causes further unemployment, in a vicious circle.

Many prominent analysts of the European social model reject any characterization of these economic pressures as implying a crisis. Instead, they talk about reform, rationalization, and self-adjustment of the welfare state, where the EMU is, if anything, a contributor to stability, as opposed to an underlying cause of a crisis. Martin Rhodes (2002: pp. 311–312) points to the "remarkable continuity" of social expenditure levels in the 1990s, in relation to previous decades. He also argues that the empirical evidence does not justify the fear of "social dumping," where economic competition from less-developed welfare states in southern (and now also eastern) Europe would compel the northern European welfare states to "retrench" in a "race to the bottom." As a close observer of the Mediterranean, he argues, rather, that there is evidence of a "race to the top," insofar as the southern welfare states—notably, Portugal—have extended coverage to more groups who previously were not protected by a safety net (pp. 319–320; see also Moreno, 2000). Furthermore, the EMU and the GSP have increased the *need* and the *scope* for strengthening the corporatist collective agreement and industrial relations regime. The need has increased because this is one of the few areas where nation-states can recover some economic-policy autonomy. The scope for agreements has simultaneously increased, since the reduction of policy tools under the formal discretion of the state has limited the scope for distributive conflict between the social partners. Social pacts also reemerged in the 1990s throughout the EU, after a decade of corporatist decline in the 1980s (Rhodes, 2002: pp. 324, 327; Hemerijck, 2002: pp. 11–12). According to Rhodes, fiscal consolidation for the purpose of meeting the Maastricht convergence criteria was largely achieved through reduced interest payments. Such payments were caused by reduced-risk premiums that could be "imported" to previously high-inflation countries from the low-inflation countries in the EMU core through the common currency backed by the GSP's credibility. This even had positive demand-side effects via decreasing interest rates. In addition, fiscal consolidation was largely secured on the revenue side. True, corporate taxation rates and employers' contributions were reduced. However, tighter write-off rules for corporate taxes, and the switching from payroll surcharges to general taxation, increased the tax base. In addition, privatization increased state revenue (Rhodes, 2002: pp. 317–318).

These contributions demonstrate that the relationship between the EMU and welfare-state retrenchment is complex. For one, the welfare state is an institution that is, as argued above, intertwined with and constitutive of the very being of modern European social order. Hyperbolic claims of an outright end of the welfare state are out of order in the foreseeable future. Furthermore, consistent with the previous chapter and the argument about uneven development and agglomoration economies, it is possible that in some locales the welfare state has been maintained at existing levels and perhaps even expanded. But, the implications for *social citizenship* conveyed by these indicators are highly misleading. As Esping-Andersen put it in a memorable turn of phrase, it is hard to find any instance where social forces have struggled for spending, as such. "Expenditure is epiphenomenal to the substance of the welfare state" (1990: p. 19). What matters are, rather, *effective entitlements* and the extent to which they correspond to the norms of distributive justice and legitimacy contained in the social citizenship accords.

When considered from this point of view, the stability of social expenditure levels may actually be an indicator of significant welfare-state retrenchment. This is because, from the viewpoint of prevailing norms of *unchanged* social citizenship, there are good grounds to suppose that there should be an *increase* of claims. First and foremost, the European population is aging, and there has been a marked increase in pensioners ready to make claims on programs they contributed toward in their working lives. The level of claims has been exacerbated by previous rationalization strategies (in Christian-democratic welfare states) based on early retirement. Second, divorce rates have increased markedly, leading to an increase of single-parent households (mostly headed by single mothers). This, along with the efforts to increase employment rates and the aspiration of women to become full economic citizens, has increased the demand for family services. It is no wonder, then, that Rhodes's more disaggregated figures point to a marked shift of resources toward areas like these (2002: pp. 312–313).

From the vantage point of social citizenship norms, then, it makes more sense to focus on the interrelationship of welfare-state programs and what entitlements they provide. Given the increased demand for and claims on these programs, despite fixed resources, we can expect that there has been significant retrenchment. This is, indeed, born out by the evidence. Using for their research the outstandingly comprehensive comparative database of social programs at the Institute for Social Research (University of Stockholm), Joakim Palme and Walter Korpi show that there has been a marked reduction of the net replacement rates for benefits received due to sickness, work accidents, and unemployment in Europe (see also the "social reforms database" of the Fondazione Rodolfo Debendetti [2005], cited in Mabbett and Schelkle, 2005). These indicators are more transparent, since changes in the likes of pensions only have an effect after a long time lag (although it is clear that reforms, such as the ones in the French pension system, will have effects on future replacement rates [e.g., Palier, 2000]). They observe a marked decrease in these rates in the period 1975–1995 (Korpi and Palme, 2003; Korpi, 2003: p. 597). This corroborates what one would expect from changes in welfare legislation in countries of the eurozone, pointing toward retrenchment.

But above all, as Korpi (2003) rightly points out, what Hemerijck, Rhodes, and most of the "new politics of retrenchment" literature forget is that the end of both the full employment commitment and the understanding of employment in terms of a right to work at a certain standard, is *in and of itself* a crucial indicator of welfare-state retrenchment.

> [U]nemployment . . . [is] . . . a central variable [of the welfare state] . . . because for categories of citizens with labour power as their main basic power resource, the efficacy of this resource in distributive conflict and bargaining is to a major extent determined by the demand for labour and by the level of unemployment. . . . [T]he maintenance of low levels of unemployment empowers citizens and is an essential preventative part of the welfare state. . . . In western Europe, the emergence of full employment as well as the expansion of social transfers and social services . . . emerged approximately at the same time. . . . [C]ontemporaries saw this triplet as constituting a unity, the full employment welfare state, where expanding social insurance and services were combined with unemployment rates below the 3 percent maximum level set by the British social reformer William Beveridge. . . . It was a manifestation of what can be called an implicit social contract between the main interest groups in these countries. . . . The return of mass unemployment must be seen as . . . the eradication of one of the corner stones of the western European welfare states. (pp. 592, 593–594, 596)

In light of this, it is not surprising that inequality levels also increased in the 1990s, nor that there have been serious cutbacks to public services in relation to demand (Clayton and Pontusson, 1998). It is also not surprising, looking at matters in a longer-term time scale, that the almost perfect proportionality of social-wage increases with economic growth has been broken, indicating that the wage relation is increasingly defined as a "market variable," as opposed to a means to disseminate the "fruits of progress" and to ensure the "virtuous" Fordist relationship between, inter alia, mass production, productivity growth, and mass consumption (Boyer, 1995). Thus, it is also doubtful whether the corporatist bargains of the 1990s really represent continuity, or even "self-transformation." In contrast to previous periods, when the raison d'être of corporatist bargains was to contain price increases at full employment, they are now used in order to secure wage settlements below rates of productivity growth at high unemployment levels. Unions have signed onto these "bargains" from a position of exceptional weakness in order to increase—but not guarantee—the probability that their doing so will boost employment. This puts serious strain on the "moral economy" that makes workers join unions in the first place, as unions are perceived to contain rather than increase wages, and as concessions put strains on union democracy at the expense of peak-level concertation. All of these problems are exacerbated when the bargains *fail* to boost employment significantly, since they contribute to the dynamic of competitive austerity, as analyzed in the previous chapter (Ryner and Schulten, 2003; Bieling and Schulten, 2003).

When matters are considered at the more disaggregated level of entitlement, Rhodes does concede that there has been significant retrenchment. There has been some increase of inequality, mainly due to increased incidence of aging, single parenthood, and unemployment. Also, while Portugal, Spain, and Italy have mainly rationalized in terms of a redistribution of entitlements, it is conceded that in France, Germany, Belgium, and Austria important changes in entitlements have occurred that are more or less directly linked to the Maastricht convergence criteria. In Finland, the Netherlands, and Ireland, such changes preceded Maastricht (Rhodes, 2002: pp. 318–322). And, indeed, it is conceded that there clearly have been adverse deflationary effects on employment rates (p. 305). The point they make, though, is that these are seen as necessary changes, and the EMU has served as a catalyst for this "necessary retrenchment" in order to put European welfare states on a more secure footing. It is in this sense that the EMU has been "good" for the European welfare state.

There are at least two problems with this argument. First, the political economy of welfare-state restructuring is interpreted in an extremely deterministic way as taking place against the backdrop of a condition of postindustrialism, which imposes a logic of "no alternative" to entitlement retrenchment. EMU is then seen as beneficial for the welfare state as a catalyst for making social groups see sense and participate in the policy process of adjustment (Hemerijck, 2002: pp. 3–9; Rhodes, 2002: pp. 308, 311, 318).

We have already encountered the postulation of a postindustrial dilemma in Chapter 3. It is derived from a simple, two-sector model developed in the 1960s by the economist W. Baumol (1967). To recall the substance of the argument: As industrialization progresses, the manufacturing sector becomes increasingly capital intensive and sheds labor. This labor surplus can only be absorbed by an emerging service sector. However, it is held that services, by their very nature, are not associated with the same kind of scope for continuous productivity growth as industrialized manufacturing. This means that wage and benefit rates in the service sector cannot match those of the manufacturing sector, at least at "normal" rates of profit. This has sharpened policy trade-offs; and a thorny "trilemma" has emerged, where it is becoming impossible to obtain all three conditions of low unemployment, income equality, and fiscal balance (Iversen and Wren, 1998). Analysts agree that in this situation, the Christian-democratic (and Mediterranean) welfare-state type characteristic of the eurozone is facing particularly severe crisis tendencies. This "social-insurance state," with high wage and nonwage labor costs, the latter of which are exacerbated as unemployment (and claims on social insurance) increases, is simply pricing the production factor labor out of the market—which then fiscally destabilizes the entire welfare system. In this environment, it is impossible to develop a sizable service economy, since high wage costs serve as a severe barrier to entry. In contrast to the residual-liberal state type, there is insufficient flexibility in terms of allowing wage dispersion and hence sufficiently cheap labor power for a market-based service economy. In contrast to the social-democratic welfare state, there are not sufficient tax-financed investments in social services and in active labor-market policies to expand public-sector service employment in, for example, health- and childcare, as it is assumed that these needs are best served through traditional institutions such as the family (Esping-Andersen, 1990: pp. 191–220; 1996; 1999: pp. 99–142; Hemerijck, 2002: p. 9). However, according to Hemerijck, the experience of the 1990s has demonstrated that reform is nevertheless possible. Corporatist understanding provides a way out. This understanding concerns the need to contain wage costs *as well as* accept wage segmentation, in order to achieve a measure of liberal wage flexibility, combined with Scandinavian-inspired emphasis on active labor-market policy (under the heading "reactivation")—as opposed to passive unemployment benefits. In this context, the discipline imposed by the EMU has served as a catalyst (Hemerijck, 2002: p. 9; Rhodes, 2002: p. 311). The Dutch experience, in particular, is here held up as a model to emulate.

Upon closer inspection, then, significant retrenchment is not denied; rather, it is argued that there has been an adjustment to unavoidable, objective circumstances beyond sociopolitical control. But this somewhat Malthusian view is flawed. First, as already demonstrated in Chapter 3, it is rendered problematic on an empirical level by significant instances of productivity growth in economies with significant service sectors, such as the United States, but also in Scandinavia. This suggests that there is also a difficulty of a more conceptual nature. First and foremost, the blanket term "services" is problematic for capturing diverse activities ranging from investment banking, legal advice, and marketing to haircutting, computer maintenance, healthcare, and childcare. Quite a few of these activities actually contribute to productivity growth indirectly and/or find mechanisms through which to charge the manufacturing-sector clients for these services (whether in the form of fees or taxation). Finally, services can provide demand that triggers further productivity in manufacturing, in complex "systems of innovation" (Mahon, 1987; 2007). As already argued in Chapter 3, viewed from this perspective, there is no reason to suppose that a new phase of capitalist growth in output and productivity, based on communications and computer technology, is not possible after the Fordist phase, provided that an adequate and coherent institutional framework—or mode of regulation—is instituted. It was exactly the point of the last chapter that the nature of the EMU is part of the problem, rather than the solution, in forging such a mode of regulation.

There is, in other words, no reason to suppose an objective, hyper-structural, postindustrial constraint beyond EMU-induced self-limitation impeding the expansion of social consumption and general taxation in order to boost public service–sector employment, provide childcare, healthcare, and service for the elderly and one-parent households. These are measures that would increase tax receipts, reduce claims on social insurance, and most likely also contribute to productivity growth through what in the previous chapter was termed "Kaldor-Verdoorn effects." If nothing elese, niche strategies in Scandinavia provide prima facie evidence of the plausibility of this. Rhodes is aware of this option, but argues that there was "little scope" for such expansion due to "fiscal overload" (2002: p. 319). But, inadvertently, this makes our point. The reduction of scope is institutional and due to structural social power relations, since it is determined by the GSP, the monetarist terms of the EMU, and, in the last instance, the subordination of the euro to the dollar through global financial markets.

The alternative is to pursue a more "Anglo-Saxon approach." However, as also indicated in the previous chapters, the relative validity of the eurosclerosis argument is spurious; moreover, the success of the US economy has depended on expansive demand. While one should not rule out the possibility that the kinds of solutions accounted for by Rhodes and Hemerijck will address some of the more acute unemployment problems and fiscal imbalances in the short to medium term, especially in locales where successful niche strategies have been pursued, it is unlikely that these would be the bases of a long-term solution.

The second problem with the idea of a successful self-adjustment of the European welfare state facilitated by the EMU has to do with the definition of "self." At what moment does retrenchment challenge the very quality and identity of the social citizenship accord? This is not a question that can be answered in the abstract, and most certainly it cannot be answered simply with reference to budgetary balances and internal systems logics. Rather, it depends on the extent to which reforms can also be rendered compatible with the terms of legitimacy in broader civil society. Here, the problem is that an essentially neoliberal project has been presented in mass political discourse as compatible with social citizenship and the European social model. The next section will concern itself with the tensions that are generated in the mechanisms and channels that link civil and political society; namely, the interstices between public and welfare policy reform, mass interest intermediation, and mass electoral politics.

Welfare Reform and the Crisis of Sociopolitical Representation

Given the increased importance of social citizenship, it is a fundamental characteristic of European societies in modern times that substantive distributive outcomes are central to broader sociopolitical legitimacy. These outcomes derive their importance from the breakdown of the traditional reproductive networks of community and social order, discussed above. Not only did this development give rise to the "need" for a welfare state to ensure reproductive functions, it also undermined the "self-evidence" of existing authority structures and hierarchies (Habermas, 1975). Writing with a particular concern for the legal order, Roberto Unger (1976: pp. 196–197) specifies clearly these relationships:

> Changes in the theoretical understanding of language, in the character of common beliefs about the basis and scope of legitimate state action, and in the structure of the rank order all seem to play a part. Language is no longer credited with the fixity of categories and the transparent representation of the world that would make formalism plausible in legal reasoning or in ideas about justice. In the absence of belief in the naturalness of existing hierarchies of power or distribution, the legitimacy of governmental, including judicial, activity comes to depend increasingly on the welfare consequences of that activity. Finally, the vicissitudes of class struggle strip the state of every pretense to impartiality and transform it into an acknowledged tool of factional interest in a social situation in which the dictates of justice are still believed to be unknowable.

As also indicated above, the ways in which different welfare states deal with the problem of substantive legitimacy depend on the nature of the distributive bargains between classes and social forces that underpin those states (ranging from social-democratic reformism to liberal residualism). In the Christian-democratic regime, quintessential to most of the eurozone, social legitimacy is ensured through a religiously inspired politics of mediation. This politics seeks to *restore* the legitimacy of hierarchies and authorities in a modern society, but at the same time mitigate the salience of the political cleavages they generate. It is exactly the role of the welfare state to do this, and as such it also provides the "natural party of government" with a fundamental power resource (van Kersbergen, 1995). However, in the context of a political economy of austerity that, as we contend, has resulted from the institutionalization of the EMS and the EMU, the scope of such a politics of mediation has decreased.

Van Kersbergen (1995: pp. 235–246) himself has suggested that we are witnessing the beginning of such a crisis of Christian democracy. As European societies have become secularized, Christian democracy becomes increasingly reliant on reproducing the power resources connected to the institutions it has created; namely, the welfare state. In such a situation, economic stagnation and austerity are particularly damaging for a social order defined by Christian-democratic norms, as the welfare institutions put under threat by such stagnation and austerity are intimately connected to the very stability of the social and political order itself. This section will explore in more detail how these dynamics are playing themselves out in the two largest core member states often held to form the engine of EU politics, France and Germany.

France

In France, the relationship between social welfare, social citizenship, and legitimacy is based on a particular meaning of the norm *solidarité,* which corresponds with the concern, noted above, of counteracting the disintegrative tendencies of capitalism while still harnessing its productive powers. Institutionally, this crystallized into France's particular social accord, as expressed first at the foundation of the Third Republic in 1875 and then in post–World War II welfare legislation, such as the *ordonnance du 4 octobre 1945.* As such, in the French Republican tradition, *solidarité* and welfare legislation are seen as essential to eliminate the distinction between "active" and "passive" citizenship (where the former was reserved for the wealthy and educated, who had a measure of leisure to participate in the public sphere). This distinction had marred French politics during the first century after the revolution of 1789, a century characterized by an unremitting pendulum movement between revolution and reaction, open social conflict and civil war (Beland and Hansen, 2000: pp. 50–51).

The institutions and dominant norms of *solidarité* correspond to the typical Christian-democratic principle of restoration of social order, albeit with a modernist, Durkheimean inflection. As is the case with the latter's concept of "organic solidarity," it is based on the idea of modern life as characterized by an intrinsic interdependence arising from division of labor and functional differentiation. This interdependence necessitates a system of social protection, founded on the principle of insurance, to neutralize the random risks inherent in industrial life (Beland and Hansen, 2000: p. 51). Again, the welfare state is not primarily understood in redistributive terms and even less in terms of charity. Rather, the French welfare state is very much based on social insurance and the principle of incomes replacement; programs which, while for the most part compulsory, are occupationally differentiated and managed by the social partners. The state steers the system indirectly by setting benefit and contribution levels as well as by providing supervision (Palier, 2000: p. 116).

As in most OECD countries, the welfare system was an integral part of the Fordist mode of regulation, helping sustain demand expansion, economies of scale, and full employment, all of which provided the economic surplus required to underwrite spending and commitments for healthcare, unemployment insurance, family benefits, and a pay-as-you-go pension system. But, as noted above, severe imbalances have developed in a socioeconomic context characterized by slow output and productivity growth and low employment rates. In short, increased claims and fewer contributors have led to recurrent social security deficits since 1973; that is, since the period of Fordist crisis, and the breakdown of Bretton Woods (Palier, 2000: pp. 116–117; Clark, 2001). In addition, due to a marked increase of long-term structural unemployment, an ever-larger proportion of the population never qualify for employment-related programs and thus are excluded from coverage (Palier, 2000: pp. 127–128; Levy, 2001). Due to the failed takeoff of a "new European economy," these imbalances remain and have been exacerbated. At the same time, governments have continuously argued that modernization measures entailed by the SEM, the EMS, and the

EMU may require short-term sacrifices, but that these measures ultimately are intended to ensure the survival of these systems by reviving economic growth. However, as stagnation continues, a profound contradiction remains between policy reforms and the terms of social legitimacy and political representation.

Because of the persistent efficacy of the norms of *solidarité* in France, the institutional persistence of expectations (social-insurance contributions are understood as a deferred wage, and any reduction of coverage is easily construed as a break of the social contract), and the entrenched status of interest groups in the system, political elites face severe constraints in any attempt to retrench the system in the wake of neoliberal imperatives. To be sure, French presidentialism seems to give the state more executive authority to take hard decisions. But there are powerful countervailing forces: the dual-executive nature of the French system; electoral laws that encourage the formation of composite coalitions; and the semiautonomous status given to professional groups and unions in managing French social insurance, connected to the Jacobin tradition of street protests when the executive is seen as having gone too far. French unions and other social movements have time and again demonstrated their capacity and skill in strategically harnessing such outbursts, in a practice referred to as *greviculture*—that is, the "gardening of grievances" (Palier, 2000; Ross, 2004).

Indicative of this constraint is the fact that, in the 1970s and 1980s, political elites of all political persuasions preferred to deal with fiscal imbalances by increasing contribution rates rather than reducing benefit levels (let alone suggesting a dismantling of the system) (Palier, 2000: pp. 118–121). The end result was an increase of the rate of social expenditure, tending toward Scandinavian proportions, financed directly by payroll taxes that added to labor costs.

But by the early 1990s, this strategy started to reach its limits. Sluggish growth and high unemployment rates persisted at the same time as demographic trends made the situation increasingly acute in the pension regime. In addition, the Treaty of Maastricht had just been signed, with the requirements associated with the Maastricht convergence criteria. It was in this context that the Gaullist prime ministers Balladur and Juppé took initiatives to reduce replacement rates. The failure of the Juppé plan in 1995 has become emblematic as an expression of the popular resistance in France to neoliberal deepening. The strikes that followed, with popular appeal, are seen as a formative moment of the antiglobalization movement. Having reneged on Chirac's explicit promises in the presidential elections of the same year, Juppé premised his strategy on the strong executive powers derived from the Gaullists' control of the presidency as well as the National Assembly. In other words, in a move that has been described as "Bonapartist" (Vail, 1999), Juppé, relying on the comparative autonomy of the French state, attempted to force through unpopular reforms. But after six weeks of popularly backed strikes, the government backed down and Juppé never recovered. Chirac called National Assembly elections one year early, which the left won.

The centerpiece of the Juppé plan was a reform of public-service pensions, extending the qualifying period from 37.5 to 40 years of service, and extending the time period over which the reference salary of pensions is calculated, from the average of the best 10 to the best 25 years. Ironically, this plan was based on a template of a private pension reform that Juppé's more cautious predecessor, Balladur, had managed to implement in 1993. Balladur's reform was based on careful consultation and a divide-and-rule strategy between the conflicting interests of professional groups and unions (Vail, 1999). Balladur also tended to announce his plans prior to consultation, to gauge the popular mood. If protests erupted, he would withdraw proposals. He avoided provocative changes of principle, such as the proposal of the Juppé plan that social-security budgets become subject to a vote in the National Assembly, challenging the authority of the social partners in their management. However, conversely, organized interests in France soon caught on to Balladur's method, mobilizing protests at every proposal, thus immobilizing his retrenchment plans. The end result was that the Gaullist governments of the 1990s were caught between the acute legitimation problems of the Juppé plan and the paralyzation of Balladur's (Levy, 2001: pp. 267–271).

The debacle of the Juppé administration and the 1997 election resulted in cohabitation between the Gaullist president Chirac and a Socialist-led coalition government headed by Lionel Jospin. The Jospin government was also caught in the bind between economic structural and institutional imperatives, and imperatives of legitimation. Almost immediately, it reneged on promises to pursue reflationary policies and to challenge the terms of the EMU, and it signed the Amsterdam Treaty. Jospin presided over a series of austerity budgets and more privatization initiatives than all previous right-wing governments combined, as well as over labor-market reform. However, in all these instances, he accompanied the new moves with compensatory policies. Labor-market reform went hand in hand with the thirty-five-hour week; retrenchment of social insurance was always targeted toward the well-to-do (and core constituencies of the right). In particular, means testing was introduced for family allowances. Increased controls and constraints were introduced for supplementary health insurance provision. The government was also keen to involve unions in tripartite negotiations over the terms of privatization and offered measures of retraining and labor-market policy (Levy, 2001: pp. 271–275). In addition, on the European level, his government worked to further European economic government as a counterweight to the ECB.

Overall, the most significant legacy of the Jospin government has been a relative shift from a welfare state based on income replacement, to more of an emphasis on means testing for the less-well-to-do. A major health reform extended health coverage. This followed an increased emphasis on the means-tested guaranteed minimum allowance—previously introduced by the Rocard government in 1988—which targeted programs for youth unemployment. The problem with these reforms is that they do not accord with the terms of the French social contract of *solidarité,* which assumes that risks are random and can affect all (Beland and Hansen, 2000). Hence, the welfare state is a concern for all. The classical problem with means testing is that it runs the risk of breaking the social bond of welfare-state consensus, as measures are increasingly seen as being designed for targeted minority groups. This tends to attenuate the willingness of people to pay contributions at the same time as they seek private alternatives. In addition, as means testing is associated with alienating surveillance, and generally is inadequate in dealing with social deprivation (such as long-term unemployment), they do not generate enthusiastic support from the targeted groups (e.g., Offe, 1997).

Ultimately, Jospin's Janus-faced attempts to combine neoliberalism with welfarism was a political failure, as he resoundingly lost to Jean-Marie Le Pen in the first round of the 2002 presidential elections. The governing concept clearly failed in holding together a heterogeneous left-wing alliance, and the left vote fragmented badly, with two Trotskyite parties taking important votes from the government parties. In addition, Le Pen's Front Nationale has been very successful in picking up urban, white working-class votes throughout the 1980s and 1990s from the Communists and the Socialists (Davies, 2002: pp. 140–143). The Gaullist government, which was subsequently elected with little enthusiasm, is greatly aware of the very delicate politics of representation that resulted from the attempts to mediate neoliberal austerity measures with the terms of legitimacy in French civil society in the 1990s. As a result, it was in no mood to renege on promises of tax cuts to meet the terms of the GSP in 2003.

At the same time, against the backdrop of continuing sluggish growth and high unemployment, serious strains in the French variant of social citizenship continue to manifest themselves in dramatic events. In 2005 widespread riots among long-term unemployed youths demonstrated that social exclusion was a growing problem. In the aftermath of the riots France voted decisively against the Constitutional Treaty. In 2006 (and following the pattern of the Juppé reforms a decade earlier), mass protests forced Prime Minister de Villepin to withdraw legislation intended to decrease social protection and employment rights. The victory of Nicolas Sarkozy in the presidential elections of May 2007, celebrated by big business and bourses across the European continent, indicated a sharp turn to the right. Through his appeals to "law and order" Sarkozy managed to mobilize considerable support among industrial workers in the north who had previously supported Jean-Marie Le Pen after having been abandoned by a Socialist Party that was unable to combine market integration with a social dimension.

Sarkozy's project of "renewal," which includes a reorientation toward the United States, illustrates the close relationship between neoliberalism and Atlanticism, a subject that we explore in greater detail in Chapter 5. However, his attempts to introduce neoliberal reforms will necessarily be selective and highly contested in both the European and national arenas. The desire to cut taxes will conflict with France's obligations under the GSP while any sustained bid for demand-led growth will collide with the macroeconomic imperatives of the ECB. These factors suggest the possibility of future conflicts with Brussels and Berlin. Indeed, mercantilist and anti-ECB rhetoric was central to Sarkozy's campaign. A Thatcherite project will not be replicated easily in France, which remains dependent on its strong industrial base and cannot embrace globalization wholeheartedly. Notwithstanding the diminished strength of the left, large numbers of French are not convinced that deregulated labor markets are in their interest.

Germany

In contrast to France, (West) Germany had a much less problematic relationship with the EMS, since it, in effect, dictated the terms of the latter as part of a strategy of adaptation to the post–Bretton Woods era. The terms of the EMU were also forged on the basis of German dominance, with the aim to ensure continuity with the EMS. As we have seen in earlier parts of this book, the particular configuration of the German export sector played a central role in this context. But, as we have also seen, changes in that sector mean that these conditions no longer obtain. As a result, since the late 1990s, the German mass parties find it increasingly difficult to pursue successful electoral and governance strategies that reproduce the social coalitions underpinning them. There is strong evidence that these difficulties are connected to welfare state retrenchment and reform, which German governments have seen themselves as forced to implement in the wake of the economic stagnation and high unemployment that we attribute to EMU-led competitive austerity (see Chapter 3).

Germany is, with good reason, described as the quintessential Christian-democratic welfare state (Clasen, 1994), with roots in the emblematic Bismarck social reforms of the 1880s. The German welfare state rests on two pillars. First, the collective bargaining regime recognizes employers' organizations and trade unions as "factors of social order," and the coverage of collective agreements forged at a sectoral level is generalized to all labor-market contracts, for union as well as nonunion members. This is so that, according to prevailing and underlying sociopolitical norms, economic efficiency and social justice as well as security and order can be reconciled. Second, social policy is almost exclusively composed by social-insurance and transfer payments. This system is highly segmented into many particular but compulsory funds, organized according to status and profession. The underlying principle of the system is status- and profession-specific social protection through incomes replacement in case of unemployment, old age, injury, and illness, funded according to the pay-as-you-go principle. Entitlements are a function, then, of active employment. German social policy is based on the male-breadwinner model, where one-earner family households are assumed and encouraged. Provision for public services, such as childcare, are poorly developed. It is generally assumed that those with social needs, who cannot claim social insurance on the basis of past employment, are dependent on other family members, relatives, or at least a local community (the subsidiarity principle). Only when it is demonstrated that these support networks have failed can social assistance be granted, through means testing.

As argued above, these institutions proved to be successful not only in facilitating the "German economic miracle" in the Fordist period. The German model also proved to be remarkably successful in reconciling the social market with monetarism in the post–Bretton Woods era, through a successful export-oriented niche strategy. Since the external and economic dimensions of this have already been discussed, we will now elaborate on the social and distributive side. Instead of relying on Keynesian pump-priming (which never played much of a role in Germany), since the oil crises and the collapse of Bretton Woods in the 1970s the German welfare state depended on corporatist productivity bargains between organized labor and business, within the framework of a supportive state. In this way, high wages were secured over the sectors, in exchange for labor quiescence in the face of rapid technological change and innovation in the workplace—securing productivity growth and competitiveness in high quality and value-added sectors. Insofar as this resulted in higher capital intensity and labor shedding, the social-insurance systems played an important role in the way that Germany accommodated itself to the new situation in the emergent US neoliberal and minimal hegemonic framework. Those who were laid off were compensated generously through, in the first instance, early-retirement packages and unemployment insurance. These, in turn, were underwritten by the productivity bargains.

Up until the mid-1990s, this was a much-admired model, which seemed to represent a progressive competitiveness, a supply-side alternative to Thatcherism and Reaganism. However, it has a number of downsides. It is fundamentally dependent on high output and productivity growth, on whether or not the export sector remains competitive (which the German export sector does), and on the capacity to tax this sector in order to fund the compensatory arrangements. This model is becoming increasingly difficult to sustain. Not long after the ink had dried on the ratified Maastricht Treaty in 1993, Germany belatedly entered the world recession of the early part of that decade, and it has never returned to its impressive growth rates of the past. It seems as if reliance on this type of supply-side economics has reached its limits and that its compensatory mechanisms are becoming overloaded. This is progressively undermining the equation between the social market and the monetarist terms, which constituted the very social foundation of Germany's accommodation to US minimal hegemony.

The German slowdown of the 1990s coincided with and exacerbated the effects of two other important secular trends and a monumental formative event. The first secular trend is the aging of the German population, which is further increasing the stress on the pension system. The second secular trend is the challenge to traditional gender roles and to the traditional family, which is undermining the male-breadwinner model and the corresponding welfare model. In particular, this is further contributing to unemployment as women enter the workforce, and it is increasing demand for public supports (such as childcare facilities and social assistance for single-parent families) as the family as a support structure is eroding. The monumental formative event is, of course, German reunification, which was pursued in the form of an extension of the Federal Republic of Germany. This resulted in massive deindustrialization and unemployment rates, which were addressed through an extension of West German social-insurance programs to the population of the East. Very quickly, the nonwage labor costs required to fund social insurance increased to 40 percent of total labor costs, while unemployment rates skyrocketed (Streeck and Trampusch, 2005). It seems, then, that the mechanisms and strategy through which Germany's still-welfarist social accords were accommodated to neoliberalism have been exhausted.

The overload of the compensatory mechanisms that worked so well in the 1970s and 1980s can be captured by what Streeck and Trampusch (2005: p. 4) call a "vicious circle of positive feedback" between high nonwage labor costs and unemployment. The high nonwage labor costs make German labor more expensive, and German workers must demand higher gross wages in order to improve their disposable income. This induces firms to shed labor and increase capital intensity, and this increases nonwage labor costs further, because the claims on the pay-as-you-go transfer systems increase further, which in turn requires higher social contribution rates.

Against this backdrop, Helmut Kohl's government introduced a consolidation package in 1997 that amounted to "the largest cutbacks in social policy in the Federal Republic's history" (Siegel, 2004: p. 118). It included retrenchment of disability pensions and reduction of benefits and tightening of eligibility criteria for unemployment insurance, as well as abandonment of the parity principle (equal share of the financial burden between labor and capital) in health insurance. The last proposal represented a major departure from the German model. In addition, the consolidation package introduced a whole host of changes to the pension system; among them, the retirement age for women was increased from sixty to sixty-five. Most significantly, though, the Kohl government changed the principle of pension provision, away from the German pay-as-you-go principle, where benefit levels determined the revenue to be raised. It was changed in an actuarian direction, so that benefits would depend on revenues. On the basis of "the demographic factor," it was estimated that the effect of this would be a reduction of the replacement rate from 70 percent to 64 percent by 2030 for a "standard pensioner" with forty-five years of uninterrupted, full-time employment to her or his credit. Procedurally, this reform broke with the established tripartite principle, as the government introduced the reforms unilaterally, without consulting the social partners (Manow, 1997: p. 32; Streeck and Trampusch, 2005: p. 9). This consolidation was to create the fiscal space, within the terms of the Maastricht convergence criteria, for a reduction of income and corporate taxes.

Subsequent political developments illustrate vividly the complex and decidedly welfarist nature of the terms of legitimacy in German political society and in the public sphere that constrains the prospects for further neoliberal deepening. Politically, the 1997 reforms provided a rallying point for the SPD/Green opposition, which vowed to repeal them, and they contributed significantly to the change of government in the 1998 elections (Schuldi, 2002: p. 153, cited in Streeck and Trampusch, 2005: p. 9; Siegel, 2004).

The reforms seriously constrained the capacity of the Christian Democratic Union (CDU) and its Bavarian "sister party," Christian Social Union (CSU), to pursue successfully the politics of mediation required in a Christian-democratic polity. German mass parties (*volksparteien*) are dependent on appealing to a wide range of identities, groups, and interests, and when in government, managing to reconcile this pluralistic and potentially contradictory mix with operational policies that are consistent with the term of socioeconomic structures (Häusler and Hirsch, 1989). The CDU/CSU, as the German "natural party of government," has been particularly successful in doing so in the postwar period, compared to its rival Party of Democratic Socialism (SPD). During the early era of the Kohl government, this party managed to reproduce, through its party politics, an alliance of market-oriented neoliberal forces, with value-conservative, rightist populist elements. But the secret of its electoral success was its capacity to recapture Catholic working-class voters (in export-competitive sunrise sectors in southern Germany) from the SPD of Brandt and Schmidt. Finally, it managed to recapture the vote of the bourgeois center—white-collar professionals who assign a great degree of value to the welfare state but also to economic competence. (This was, in many respects, symbolized by Free Democratic Party's [FDP] change of allegiance from the SPD to the CDU as coalition partner in the early 1980s.) The height of the CDU's success in managing the politics of mediation was in the first election after reunification, when it managed to bring in the vast majority of the Eastern German electorate into its coalition (Schmid, 1998).

In the aftermath of the 1997 welfare reforms, the SPD, the Greens, and the PDS (the Party of Democratic Socialism in East Germany) managed to win back the bourgeois center and East German voters by persuading these strata of society that they would be better at reconciling economic innovation with social justice. And, while the SPD and Greens were less than successful in making inroads among Catholic workers in the south, they reconciled this appeal to a "new center" with a high degree of mobilization of their core working-class vote in the country's northwestern industrial heartland (Lösche and Walter, 1992; Ryner, 2003). But the challenge that the "red-green" government failed to meet was that of successfully rendering this coalition compatible with a sustainable and coherent concept of socioeconomic governance.

In order to pursue an alternative economic policy, consistent with its 1998 electoral pledges to restore the terms of the German social accord challenged by Kohl's 1997 reforms, there were two potential—and potentially mutually supportive—strategies that the red-green coalition could possibly have pursued.

The first of these was broadening the tax base, to move away from a mode of financing that was imposing the highest possible burden on variable labor costs. In other words, this would have been a reform away from financing through *employment* surcharges toward *general* taxation, with the aim of encouraging more labor intensity in the economy while maintaining the fiscal capacity to meet existing social-insurance commitments. However, as Streeck and Trampusch (2005: pp. 22–23) point out, this is a more difficult strategy to pursue than one might think. First, existing social-insurance commitments in Germany are already, to a large extent, funded indirectly through general taxation, since the systems have become highly dependent on a complex web of federal subsidies. Second, especially in an environment of retrenchment, the social partners, especially the trade unions, do not trust the shift of fiscal authority to what it considers to be the vagaries of party politics. Thirdly, such a social-democratic move would face the highly ingrained conservative principle of equivalence (that there is a proportional relationship between what you put in and what you get out of the system). All those challenges would be easier to meet if the revenue to be raised would significantly contribute toward maintaining existing commitments, but this would, according to these authors, run into the constraint that supplies the central theme of this book:

> In any case, the first priority for the Federal Government is *balancing* its budget, not *expanding* it. The main criterion by which the performance of the Finance Minister is publicly judged year by year is whether his budget meets the targets of the Maastricht stability pact. (Streeck and Trampusch, 2005: p. 22)

This, then, leads to the second possible strategy that could have been pursued, namely challenging the terms upon which the EMU and the GSP were based. Such a strategy would have served to boost the sluggish demand side of the German economy in order to promote demand-led growth of output and productivity, which we have characterized as "Kaldor-Verdoorn effects."

The red-green government pursued elements of these two strategies at various times but with insufficient resolve and coherence, no doubt exacerbated by perceived external constraints and internal divisions, as symbolized in the early days of the government by the rivalry between Chancellor Gerhard Schröder and the party chairman and finance minister, Oskar Lafontaine. True, the red-green government repealed the Kohl retrenchments of 1997, introduced an ecological tax (as part of a more comprehensive tax reform aimed at lower corporate taxation in exchange for fewer write-offs), and reduced income taxes for low- and middle-income earners. It was assumed that the income and growth effects would make the reforms revenue-neutral. In order to secure adequate growth rates, Lafontaine started a number of initiatives on the EU stage that amounted to a call to renegotiate the terms of the Maastricht bargain. Together with his French and Italian counterparts, Lafontaine called for a more flexible interpretation of the GSP and for EU corporate tax harmonization, made explicit calls to the ECB to lower interest rates, and supported the Japanese call for target exchange-rate zones between the dollar, yen, and euro (Ryner, 2003: pp. 214–217).

Lafontaine's initiatives put the fledgling government under severe pressure from the ECB and the financial and business community, and it generated internal tensions, pitting Lafontaine against Schröder "modernizers," who had little time for his Keynesianism. It should also be pointed out that Lafontaine did not challenge the structures of transnational finance, which punished his calls by imposing a risk premium on the euro, thus making his calls for interest-rate reductions counterproductive. There is, then, not a little irony in the fact that his desire for interest-rate reductions was realized after he had resigned. After Lafontaine's resignation, the German government returned, under Hans Eichel's tenure as finance minister, to a macroeconomic stance quite reminiscent of that under Kohl.

In this situation, the red-green government soon found their initiatives for broadening the tax base insufficient, especially since they, at the same time, pursued a policy of corporate- and income-tax reduction within the terms of the Maastricht Treaty. This inevitably led them to a policy of pursuing welfare-state retrenchment, just as the Kohl government had. In 2000 and 2001, just as we have seen in France, the indexation of pensions was tied to consumer prices, as opposed to wages. Even more significantly, a "third pillar" of actuarial supplementary pensions were enacted in 2001, in order to provide relief to the pay-as-you-go system. By 2004, a "sustainability factor," another phrase for CDU's "demographic factor," was added to the pensions system, completing the circle toward the stance of the Kohl government (Streeck and Trampusch, 2005: p. 12). Unemployment benefits were originally kept more or less intact, apart from a change of indexation from wage to consumer price increases. But, after the election of 2002, the so-called Hartz I and Hartz II reforms introduced major changes. The rules for rejecting jobs on offer were tightened and low-wage employment was encouraged through exemptions from social-insurance contributions and the creation of temporary-job agencies. In 2003, Agenda 2010, with the Hartz III and IV reforms, was introduced. Agenda 2010 relaxed employment protection in small firms and shortened the duration of unemployment benefits to a general maximum of twelve months (from thirty-two months). The most radical of these reforms is, however, the amalgamation of unemployment and social assistance, which, in effect, means that long-term unemployed will be reliant on a low flat-rate and means-tested benefit—a major breach of incomes replacement norms. However, significant healthcare reform has been blocked by the Christian-democratic majority of the German upper house, representing the regions, and effective lobbying of doctors' professional associations and the pharmaceutical industry (Streeck and Trampusch, 2005: pp. 12–32; see also Seeleib-Kaiser, 2003).

Against the backdrop of these retrenchments, never thematized in general elections, the SPD suffered major electoral setbacks and found it increasingly difficult to maintain the electoral alliance it managed to forge in 1998. Its core working-class constituency became increasingly disillusioned and difficult to mobilize at election time. Against the backdrop of continued economic stagnation, as the "flexibility reforms" failed to turn the situation around, the government performed badly, both in terms of defending social protection and in terms of economic competence, the central values that attract the white-collar strata of the bourgeois center. After remaining in power with the slimmest of margins in 2002 (due to the CDU/CSU fielding such a polarizing candidate for chancellor as Edmund Stoiber, Schröder taking populist credit for his handling of the Elbe floods in the east, and opposition to the Iraq War), the SPD lost power in its very heartlands of Hamburg and North-Rhine Westphalia in 2004 and 2005, forcing an early general election in September 2005.

It was generally expected that the CDU/CSU would easily win these elections, fought together with the FDP on an agenda of neoliberal deepening. Among other things, the electoral manifesto called for a change to the collective bargaining system, where collective agreements would no longer be generalized beyond the sphere of the unionized workers—a radical departure from the tripartite system to one of enterprise corporatism. Also, the proposed candidate for finance minister suggested the possibility of a flat-rate tax system. The relative failure of the CDU/CSU appeal, especially among the long-term unemployed in the eastern parts of Germany (who clearly do not buy into the argument that increased flexibility will bring them gainful employment), is indicative that terms of legitimacy in Germany still make neoliberal retrenchment very difficult. The CDU/CSU failed to make any headway in regaining red-green votes. Instead, the lack of popularity of the red-green government translated into the considerable success of the new Left Party, created through a merger of the PDS and the Electoral Alternative for Labor and Social Justice (WASG), a protest movement that arose from disgruntled former SPD members and trade unionists, with its origins in the latest North-Rhine Westphalia elections. This party has been particularly successful in the east, where it is now the second largest party. This left-populist party seems to have filled the vacuum left by the failures of the two mass parties, and as a result thwarted—at least for now—the rise of a strong right-radical force on a federal level, which, however, has had successes in some regional elections.

Given the CDU's inability to formulate a credible alternative, the "grand coalition" under Angela Merkel is not surprising. The elites of the CDU and the SPD actually are very close to one another in their thinking about national and international problems and their solutions (see Chapter 5). This outcome does not, however, represent a stabilization of German political society. First, the reduction of the SPD/CDU vote to below 70 percent indicates a significant decline of the vote for the mass parties. Since 1990, the SPD has lost one-third of its members and only 2.8 percent of its members are under thirty (Greffrath, 2005: p. 2). Equally important is a central lesson of mainstream political sociology; namely, that it is the very competitiveness of the party system that is essential to the legitimacy of mass liberal-democratic political societies, since it "helps set the national system of government *above* any particular office holders" (italics in original) (Lipset and Rokkan, 1967: p. 92). The formation of a grand coalition represents a major attenuation of this principle, where the legitimacy of the system as such becomes much more intimately connected with the success of the office holders.

Europe Beyond the Era of Mass Parties?

Although EMU has been widely assumed to be compatible with Europe's social models, the evidence presented in this book suggests otherwise.

The welfare states of Europe are central to substantive legitimacy. They are not "options" or "luxuries," but rather constitutive elements of European democracy, painstakingly constructed out of the ashes of war and fascism, and central to the stable functioning of European capitalism. Yet, they are beginning to buckle under the pressures of neoliberal reforms spearheaded by EMU. Monetarism, labor flexibility, and fiscal retrenchment have not sparked economic recovery, but rather have served further to entrench stagnation and mass unemployment. The result has been a gathering crisis of political legitimacy that strikes at the heart of the political parties that have sustained the welfare state in the core of the eurozone. The era of mass parties appears to be drawing to a close.

The second part of this chapter provided a detailed analysis of the increased constraints that the mainstream political systems face in the two core states of the eurozone, France and Germany. The broad conclusion is that as long as these political systems and their actors continue to operate within the straitjacket set by the EMU and the (somewhat less restrictive) GSP, the contradictory compulsions toward neoliberal reform and the maintenance of a Christian-democratic welfarist legitimacy will lead to an impasse likely to further strain these systems and expand the room for maneuver of populist forces to the left and the right. In some respects, of course, this contention concurs with more conventional mainstream analyses. We sharply differ from these analyses, however, in their assumption that further doses of neoliberal reforms will provide the cure. The acquiescence of European business to the minimally hegemonic order has facilitated corporate profitability. But it has done so at the expense of domestic legitimacy and stability and, as we argue in Chapter 5, the prospects for European unity and global influence.

It is beyond the scope of the chapter to engage in a more comprehensive and general analysis of the political situation in the member states of the eurozone beyond France and Germany. Nevertheless, it is clear that the fragmentation in Germany (toward radical right-wing parties in regional elections, a new left party, and a profound tension in post-unification federalism) and France (the consolidation of the National Front [FN] and the fragmentation of the left, including the success of Trotskyite parties at the expense of the Socialist Party [PS] and the French Communist Party [PCF]) is part of a broader crisis of established parties. Examples abound in Austria, Belgium, the Netherlands, Denmark, and Italy. All of these countries exhibit, to greater or lesser degree, the diminished stature of social- and Christian-democratic parties in relation to a postmodernist phenomena: the rise of populist mavericks, reduction in voter turnout, ascendancy of personalistic or charismatic leaders, and growing volatility of electoral support. In all of these countries, moreover, extreme right-wing nationalist parties and movements have gained considerable momentum. No doubt, electoral studies and political sociologists correctly identify broad structural determinants of these phenomena. However, we believe that the more immanent cause is welfare-state retrenchment compelled by EMU-imposed austerity. Malaise at the very core of the Franco-German engine room is a profound source of instability.

5

In the Shadow of US Hegemony

Even for a senior official dealing with the US administration you are aware of your role as a tributary; however courteous your hosts you come as a subordinate bearing goodwill and hoping to depart with a blessing on your endeavors. . . . American cabinet officers arrive with the sort of entourage that would have done Darius proud. . . . Hotels are commandeered; cities brought to a halt; innocent bystanders are barged into corners by thick-necked men with bits of plastic hanging out of their ears. It is not a spectacle that wins hearts and minds.
> —Chris Patten, former European Commissioner
> for External Affairs (2006: p. 26)

The United States is a nation engaged in what will be a long war.
> —US Department of Defense (2006: p. 1)

The central theme of this book contrasts sharply with the assumptions of a gathering "European challenge" and an incipient multipolar balance of power that have informed so much recent scholarship on European and international politics. As we argue in Chapter 2, a minimalist form of US transatlantic economic hegemony emerged following the collapse of the more integral Bretton Woods system. Although beset with growing conflict and instability, the hegemonic system persists because it is underwritten by the United States' structural financial power and, as this chapter will show, US military supremacy. Chapters 2, 3, and 4 argue that transnational Western European business enjoys a privileged position within its regional domain, but plays a subordinate role within the transatlantic order. Neoliberalism, which is a constitutive part of this order, has condemned Europe to comparatively slow economic growth, high unemployment, uneven development, welfare-state retrenchment, and a deepening crisis of representation that undermine EU capacities for collective action.

Chris Patten's lament cited at the beginning of this chapter poignantly illustrates the frustrations of European politicians and diplomats in their relations with the American superpower. Grand rhetorical assertions of the EU's growing role in the world, proffered with an eye to the electoral arena, contrast with quiet acquiescence to US prerogatives, culminating in the unsuccessful attempt to cement the US political-military presence within the European constitutional order.[1] The EU has consistently failed to exert any significant moderating influence on the United States' most imperialist of postures, not least in Iraq. Even as Condoleezza Rice determined to "punish France, ignore Germany, and forgive Russia," German and French intelligence services were collaborating discretely with the US invasion of Iraq (Bernstein and Gordon, 2006: p. 1). While Defense Secretary Rumsfeld contemptuously dismissed France and Germany as "old Europe," European governments were collectively or individually facilitating hundreds of illegal and clandestine CIA flights carrying alleged terrorists to secret torture centers and permitting the United States to use European bases and airspace during the invasion of Iraq (European Parliament, 2006). Soon after the invasion of Iraq, the Franco-German-Russian "triple alliance"—based not on Kantian precepts but, rather, domestic electoral calculation and commercial interests—collapsed as Jacques Chirac began what Alain Gresh aptly called a "new romance between the Elysee palace and the White House" (2006: p. 1), while Angela Merkel became the "go to person in Europe for Washington" (*New York Times,* 2007: p. A10).

This chapter surveys the political economy of US military power in Europe since the early 1990s. The first part describes the transformation of NATO from a containment-oriented and defensive alliance to an instrument designed to promote the forward expansion of US power across the European continent and into Central Asia. We focus in this section on the catalytic effects of the wars against Serbia in 1994–1995 and 1999 on this forward expansion, the dependency resulting from Europe's growing reliance on Russian and Central Asian energy, and the limitations of the nascent European Security and Defense Policy (ESDP) in relation to the vast expansion of the US military arsenal and the militarization of US foreign policy. The United States' geopolitical advance is closely connected to the consolidation of neoliberalism on the European continent.

In the second part of this chapter, we consider the long-range possibilities for US minimal hegemony in view of formidable economic and geopolitical challenges, not least the failure of the US occupation of Iraq and the outbreak of civil war in that country. As Chapter 2 indicates, the financial underpinning of US minimal hegemony carries significant risks and vulnerabilities, which, moreover, appear to be increasing over time. The growth of deficits and dependence on foreign borrowing is the natural accompaniment to relative industrial decline and the transnationalization of production. In this context, the Bush administration's policy of geopolitical advance and militarization, designed in large part to maintain its hold over global energy resources, is a compensatory strategy (Harvey, 2003) that appears to hold growing risks and dangers. Nevertheless, although many scholars have argued that global financial disequilibrium and the disastrous Iraqi adventure portend a terminal crisis, our view is less sanguine. Despite its present difficulties, the United States retains considerable structural economic and coercive power. Without a fundamental transformation of Europe's political landscape, a precipitous crisis in the United States would be less likely to empower Europe than to exacerbate political and economic problems.

To assert that the military and economic dimensions of the transatlantic relationship are closely linked is not to imply that the role of force can always be reduced in straightforward fashion to economic factors in general, much less to the transmission of US financial hegemony and the development of neoliberalism on the European continent. To be sure, the expansion of NATO has unfolded in part according to a political-military logic that is grounded, broadly speaking, in European security concerns. The security factor has been most evident in the brutal and potentially destabilizing wars in southeastern Europe, but it is also clearly identifiable in terms of Europe's growing dependency on Russia and Central Asian and Middle Eastern energy resources.

There are two distinct senses in which it is possible to demonstrate a causal relationship between US geopolitical expansion and the consolidation of neoliberalism in Europe. In the first place, Europe's subordinate position in relation to global finance has served dramatically to widen the gap in military capabilities between the United States and Europe. The fiscal and monetary constraints of EMU have sharply limited military expenditure in the eurozone. Self-limitation and stagnation have prevented the EU from building independent security capacities. Moreover, as we show in more detail below, research and development in Europe retains a strong national component, while at the same time it has become more closely linked to the US military-industrial complex. By contrast, in the United States deficit financing has facilitated large increases in the military budget, with substantial fiscal stimulus and technological spin-offs for the US economy.

Second, the expansion of US military power across the European continent has served more specifically to reinforce the position of social forces committed to neoliberalism. Atlanticism has served as the necessary counterpart and bulwark of neoliberalism (van der Pijl, 2001). The transition from Fordism to neoliberalism in the United States and Britain, described in Chapter 2, began in the late 1970s and was consolidated under the charismatic leaderships of Thatcher and Reagan. But progress in the European continental "heartland" was slower and more reactive. As Chapter 4 argues, the sociopolitical impasse reflects in part the failure of neoliberalism to develop ideological hegemony. In his analysis of transatlantic power relations in the 1990s, Kees van der Pijl highlights the geopolitical dimension of Europe's still-incomplete transition to neoliberalism: "American offensives mobilized an Atlantic counterpart in the West European class structure" (2000: p. 279). This was foreshadowed even in the early 1980s, as the US offensive posture, including the placement of cruise and Pershing missiles, sought to block the Europeanization that was developing in the context of détente and replace it with the "Americanization of Europe" (p. 279). In a similar fashion, the US forward movement of the 1990s also served to reinforce the positions of Atlanticist and neoliberal forces. The Balkan wars—and particularly the 1999 air assault on Serbia—greatly expanded the geographical domain of neoliberalism. They also served to marginalize already weakened forces in Germany and France that were seeking to advance alternatives to neoliberalism, and to involve Atlanticist-leaning governments in Central and Eastern Europe in the US-led war. The Clinton administration made it clear to Central and Eastern European countries that NATO membership was contingent on economic reforms (Goldgeier, 1999: pp. 21–22). The resulting dual-track enlargements of NATO and the EU have solidified the relationship between Washington and social forces committed to neoliberal development strategies; the United States has acquired a stable of Trojan horses.

After the Cold War: Interregnum and Restoration of US Coercive Supremacy

US power played a central role in establishing not only the international economic and political structural conditions of the EU, but also the character of its politics, institutions, and doctrines. "Functionalism" and "neofunctionalism" reflected US academic efforts to provide an underlying intellectual rationale for European integration in the early years of the Cold War; the concept of a "United States of Europe" originated in Washington, not Paris or Bonn (Milward, et al., 1993; van der Pijl, 1996). Marshall Plan aid was instrumental in facilitating nascent forms of European supranational integration through the OEEC and European Payments Union. The European Defense Community itself was a response to US pressures for German rearmament; its failure led to direct US control over the European security architecture, through a garrison of 350,000 US troops, an archipelago of military bases, and the positioning of thousands of nuclear warheads in Western Europe, of which 480 remain in the UK, Germany, Belgium, the Netherlands, Turkey, and Italy (Norris and Kristensen, 2006: pp. 57–58).

Although important transatlantic disagreements—most notably over exorbitant monetary privileges (see Chapter 2) and the international oil regime—complicated the relationship, geopolitical weakness and fragmentation diminished the ability of Western European states individually or collectively to challenge core US interests. The Suez crisis showed that all decisions concerning the Middle East would be made in Washington, not in London or Paris. The threat to withdraw troops from Europe reinforced adherence to the dollar-gold standard during the 1960s and defeated French attempts to challenge the Anglo-US control of oil markets during the 1970s.

By eliminating its only military challenger, the collapse of the Soviet Union presented Europe with an opportunity but also a threat. The reunification of the continent appeared to establish a basis for renegotiation of Europe's political role within the transatlantic order, parallel to the formation of a monetary zone of stability. Indeed, realist scholars, who had rejected economic interpretations of the United States' postwar hegemony in Europe in favor of interpretations positing security-driven containment and power balancing, expected this outcome (e.g., Mearsheimer, 2001). Yet, the United States' drive for primacy in Central and Eastern Europe after 1991 contradicted classical realist predictions. It demonstrated the limitations of abstract, power-political perspectives that do not take social forces into account (Layne, 2006; Gowan, 2006).

The Maastricht Treaty codified ambitious plans for a common foreign and security policy (CFSP) alongside EMU. As a European constitutional process began to unfold, many observers discerned the basis of a nascent polity that was a precondition of genuine economic and geopolitical self-determination: appointment of a high representative for CFSP, expansion of the Western European Union, articulation of an ESDP involving a rapid-reaction force, agreement on a set of international humanitarian tasks, and the establishment of an EU military protectorate over Bosnia. These developments were reinforced by attempts at transnational consolidation of European defense industries (involving collaborative projects such as the Eurofighter) and the development of a European Defense Agency (EDA).

Uncertainties among US policymakers in the aftermath of 1989 also contributed to the expectation of a renegotiated multilateral political-military settlement. Residual Cold War instincts continued to influence the policies and attitudes throughout the Bush I administration and during the first years of the Clinton administration, resulting in a sphere-of-influence policy conceding considerable authority to Europe. During this brief interregnum, the United States contemplated downsizing or even eliminating NATO in favor of European security cooperation, in what appeared a replay of the European Defense Community (EDC); large-scale withdrawal of US forces to realize a "peace dividend"; and granting Russia considerable influence in Eastern Europe and the former Soviet Union. The sphere-of-influence policy seemed to accord with the Clinton administration's core project of financial liberalization, globalization, and domestic fiscal retrenchment. The first Gulf war and the UN-supervised postwar settlement temporarily reinforced these policies, reaffirming US primacy in the Middle East, albeit within the framework of coalition building and a high level of consensus among allies.

War and the Expansion of NATO

Despite Secretary of State James Baker's assurances (during negotiations with the Soviet Union over Germany's unification) that NATO would not be extended "one inch to the East" (Zelikow and Rice, 1995: p. 183), the Clinton administration abandoned the sphere-of-influence policy in favor of a forward strategy designed to expand US power over Europe and to consolidate the position of neoliberal and Atlanticist forces in individual states and in the EU as a whole (van der Pijl, 2001; Gowan, 1999).[2] The expansion of NATO was to play a central role in this transformation, whose sources were multiple and complex. They included fragmentation among the EU powers, growing disarray in southeastern Europe, the increasing importance of Eastern European economies and labor markets to the world economy, interrelationships of energy security and political stability, and the development of a more confrontational posture toward Russia.

The wars against Serbia played a central role in this transformation. Initially designated as the test case of a common EU policy, the war over Bosnia (1994–1995) would eventually demonstrate that the EU states lacked the cohesion and commitment required to fulfil their nominal ambitions, even in the European space itself, to a security order underpinned by cosmopolitan human rights norms and international law and would need to rely on US power. Confronted with pressures for structural adjustment arising from international debt exceeding $22 billion, a contraction of export markets in Western Europe, and the return of guest workers from Germany, the individual republics began to pursue their own methods of dealing with the resulting massive economic shocks, as Communist Party leaders in all of the republics underwent a seamless transition to ethnic nationalism, most notably and tragically in Serbia and Croatia. When Serb units of the Yugoslav National Army mobilized in Croatia and Slovenia, the United States accepted European Council President Jacques Poos's proclamation that "[t]his is the hour of Europe, not of America" (*Financial Times,* July 1, 1991: p. 2). Yet, Germany's recognition of Croatian and Slovenian sovereignty during the Serbo-Croat war provoked serious conflicts with France and Britain. Germany's diplomatic initiative was not linked to a broader strategy of conflict prevention and support for Bosnia, much less a broader diplomatic and political project for regional stability. Once Germany was sidelined, France and Britain offered a plan for de facto partition that rewarded, and thus further provoked, ethnic cleansing and encouraged Croatia to cooperate with Serbia (Ramet, 1996: p. 50). Massive human rights violations, the failure of UN forces to protect safe havens, and refugee flows to Western Europe generated pressures for a settlement, eventually provoking US military intervention within the framework of NATO, sponsorship of a joint Croat-Bosnian force, and culminating in the cold peace established at Dayton in 1995 (Cafruny, 2003).

Although tentative and somewhat improvisational, the US intervention in Bosnia reflected the transition in US foreign policy to a more expansionist strategy. By 1998, US policy toward southeastern Europe had begun to cohere. Although the year-long diplomatic prelude to the 1999 air war against Serbia was still marked by diplomatic uncertainty and vacillation, the United States had nevertheless moved toward a more comprehensive project for the region, predicated on the elimination of Russian influence and the establishment of an enlarged security zone under NATO control. The aerial attack on Serbia followed a period of diplomatic maneuver, establishing a more or less unified NATO stance and a propaganda offensive redefining the crisis in terms of human rights violations whose severity justified military intervention. At Rambouillet in February 1999, NATO issued an ultimatum to Serbia (and indirectly to

Russia) demanding access for NATO military deployments throughout Serbian territory. Serbia's anticipated rejection provided the basis for a 78-day bombing campaign, followed by Serbian capitulation when it became clear that Russia would not provide diplomatic or military assistance. US forces flew 80 percent of air combat missions and supplied 85 percent of munitions. The United States deployed 150 tankers, while France and Britain deployed 12 each. The war demonstrated the limitations of EU foreign and security policy and spelled the end of Russian influence in southeastern Europe.

The expansion of NATO's role "out of area" also served to buttress the position of Atlanticist forces throughout the continent, most notably in Germany. Whereas at the outset Britain and France had sought to exclude Germany from the Rambouillet negotiations, as the bombing campaign intensified, Germany emerged as a central factor in the war effort. Thus, the Blair-Schröder "third way" economic initiatives, announced at the end of the war, served to marginalize finance minister Lafontaine's compensatory policies with a modernized version of traditional social democracy (see Chapters 3 and 4). They had their counterpart in the ascendance of the Atlanticist vision of European security consolidated through the maintenance of NATO's credibility. Atlanticism was confirmed in Germany by the formal resignation and de facto ouster of Lafontaine, who had linked opposition to the war to alternatives to monetarism and Atlanticism (van der Pijl, 2001; Lafontaine, 2000).

Kosovo (along with Macedonia) has a greater significance for the international political economy than Bosnia and other parts of western former Yugoslavia. US policy since 1992 has recognized the strategic importance of Kosovo. This importance expanded greatly in the ensuing years as a result of intensifying conflicts over energy resources and the construction of pipelines linking the Caspian Sea basin to Western Europe and the Mediterranean (Baghat, 2002; Cafruny, 2003). The defeat of Serbia not only served to restore the credibility of NATO and stabilize its eastern flank, an objective that had been recognized as early as 1992, but also paved the way for the establishment of direct US military presence in the region and the concomitant transition from state capitalism to neoliberalism (Inan-Freybourg, 2005). Camp Bondsteel, built by Haliburton in 1999 as part of a $330 million contract, is the largest US military base in southeastern Europe (with permanent housing for seven thousand troops) and, together with a planned US military base in Montenegro, forms part of a virtually contiguous string of existing or projected facilities extending from the Black Sea to Afghanistan.[3] In many other respects, the war with Serbia prefigured the subsequent US invasion of Iraq and the Bush doctrine, with its emphasis on preemption, rejection of the principle of national sovereignty, and abandonment of multilateralism. Faced with Russian and Chinese opposition, the United States bypassed the UN Security Council and used humanitarian rhetoric and a NATO mandate as alternative legal and political justifications for military intervention. The heavy bombing of Belgrade and other Serb cities anticipated the "shock and awe" tactics used to subdue Baghdad and demonstrate US military prowess to the world.[4]

US Power, NATO, and "New Europe"

By the mid-1990s, the United States had moved toward a clear policy of NATO expansion in Central and Eastern Europe. The extension of US military bases and military agreements has been closely linked to EU enlargement. For all Central and Eastern European countries, membership in NATO has preceded entry into the EU.

Although the Copenhagen Criteria of 1993 formally established open-ended commitments to accession for all European countries, enlargement beyond Central Europe clearly contradicted traditional assumptions concerning the character of the EU. The wholesale expansion of the EU into Eastern Europe created de facto center-periphery relationships under the umbrella of nominal equality. If, as Chapters 2 and 3 indicate, there are serious problems in applying the concept of an "optimal currency area" to the existing eurozone, the concept is even less plausible with respect to an expanded euorzone encompassing Central and Eastern European member states. Moreover, absent the possibility of significant regional redistribution, large disparities in income and productivity make internal labor flexibility the only viable strategy for maintaining cohesion throughout the EU. Thus, although enlargement has been justified in terms of the need to promote stability and democracy in the former Soviet sphere, it has reproduced a logic of competitive austerity and uneven development in the new member states. (See Chapter 3 for a more extensive discussion of these issues.) The result has been wholesale abandonment of traditional understandings concerning the *acquis communautaire,* including some of the following changes: lengthy transition periods before allowing the free movement of labor, limitations on new member states' access to structural and CAP funds, (largely unsuccessful) attempts to limit new members' political influence. New member states have adopted economic growth strategies linked to Western European (and US) production chains and predicated on the provision of cheap labor (Gowan, 1996; Holman, 2001; Bohle, 2005). As indicated in the previous two chapters, German corporations in particular have become increasingly dependent on outsourcing; they are locating a growing share of their production to exploit lower wages in eastern Europe (Lorentowicz, Marin, and Raubold, 2002). The availability of eastern European cheap labor is a central factor in negotiations over wages and working conditions. The new member states have experienced substantial growth in inequality and continuing high unemployment (Dunford, 2005).

EU enlargement is an increasingly important component of the neoliberal concept of economic governance, but it inevitably produces internal fragmentation because it grants nominal equality to peripheral states that seek closer relations to the United States both for geopolitical reasons and because of their second-class economic and political status within the EU. As the United States struggles to maintain its primacy over the key sources of energy and transit routes in Eurasia, the development of political influence in Central and Eastern Europe has become a central aspect of US foreign policy.

European Energy, European Security, and US Power

Intensifying international competition for oil and natural gas as a result of diminishing global supplies and the rapid growth of the Chinese and Indian economies has dramatically enhanced the importance of Eurasia and the "great game" of geopolitics. Energy security has become a serious concern for European countries. The increasing significance of Eurasian sources of energy reinforces Europe's dependence on the United States. The EU currently imports 50 percent of its oil and gas, a figure that is expected to increase to 75 percent by 2030, with most supplies originating in geopolitically uncertain areas in Russia and the former Soviet Union. Germany receives 35 percent of its oil and 40 percent of its gas from Russia. Poland and Hungary import more than 60 percent of their natural gas from Russia (European Commission, 2006b: p. 1). The indirect impact on the EU of Russia's decision to cut off supplies of natural gas to Ukraine in early 2006 and oil to Belarus in early 2007, alongside Gazprom's bid to expand ownership of Western European gas companies, have dramatized Europe's energy vulnerability.

Although the European Commission has sought to promote energy liberalization, EU energy policy remains at an embryonic stage. There is no single market for energy; two decades after the advent of the Single European Act (SEA), prices for electricity and gas vary from country to country by as much as 100 percent (*Economist*, 2006a: p. 65). Despite the centrality of energy (coal) to the original European Coal and Steel Community (ECSC), there is no common EU policy of energy security. According to the European Commission, "Energy-using countries are starting to see each other as potential rivals for [energy] provision . . . just at a time when Europe imports more energy than ever before. This trend will further accelerate substantially" (*EUobserver,* 2006a: p. 1). The development of intra-European and intra-EU rivalry is evident in Russia's ability to develop long-term bilateral commercial relationships with individual member states; Italian threats to cut off energy supplies from Italy to Corsica in retaliation for France's bid to block ENEL's takeover of Suez by merging it with Gaz de France; Spain's attempt to block the takeover of Endesa by Eon of Germany; Poland's fierce opposition to the proposed German-Russian North European Gas Pipeline, a twelve-hundred-kilometer pipeline running through the Baltic Sea and bypassing Polish territory, a project Poland has compared to the Molotov-Ribbentrop Pact (Beunderman, 2006: p. 1) and subsequent threats to veto the EU-Russian Strategic Partnership Treaty; French and German opposition to Commission proposals to break up their national electricity companies, GdF and Eon; and Gerhard Schröder's appointment as director of Gazprom following the SPD's defeat in the elections of September 2005.

Although Russia enjoys considerable political leverage by virtue of its possession of oil and natural gas and its control over transport infrastructure in eastern and central Europe, it has also suffered serious political and commercial setbacks. During the mid-1990s, the major Anglo-US oil companies took advantage of Russia's weakness and passivity and made significant inroads into the Russian energy sector. Russia's reemergence as a regional power, signified by the development of nationalism and the state takeover of the Yukos empire, has enabled it to renegotiate contracts from a position of strength. Nevertheless, Russia has lost significant influence in southeastern Europe and the Black Sea region, which is the source of 50 percent of EU energy requirements and the center of transit routes connecting Central Asian and Caspian oil and gas with Western and Southeastern Europe. The US government prevented the construction of Europe's preferred crude oil pipeline from the Caspian Sea through Iran and has supported a network of alternative pipelines (financed by Anglo-US firms) that bypass Russia in their run from Central Asia to Western Europe (De Haas, 2006; Jackson, 2006).

Energy insecurity magnifies the importance of the Eurasian sphere and greatly increases Europe's dependence on US military power. US political-military initiatives in Eastern Europe are closely related to the attempt to consolidate power in the Eurasian sphere. As Zbigniew Brzezinski has written,

> Geopolitics has moved from the regional to the global dimension, with preponderance over the entire Eurasian continent serving as the central basis for global primacy. The United States . . . now enjoys international primacy, with its power directly deployed on three peripheries of the Eurasian continent serving as the central basis for global primacy. America's global primacy is directly dependent on how long and how effectively its preponderance on the Eurasian continent is sustained. (1997b: pp. 38–39)

The United States has established close bilateral relationships with strategically important Eastern European and Central Asian countries. In 2004, Kazakhstan, the largest country in Central Asia, with large and untapped oil deposits, joined the NATO-sponsored Partnership for Peace (Bordonaro, 2006a: p. 2). In April 2005, the governments of Georgia, Ukraine, Azerbaijan, and Moldova (GUAM) met with the United States to promote Euro-Atlantic integration, to incorporate Romania and Bulgaria, and to open the way for a Pax Americana extending from the Adriatic Sea to the Caspian region (Bordonaro, 2005a: pp. 3, 4). The entry of Bulgaria and Romania into NATO cemented relations with the United States prior to their accession into the EU. A similar path appeared likely for Ukraine following the Western-sponsored "Orange Revolution" of 2005, until Russia reasserted its historical influence. All of the "new European" countries strongly supported the US invasion of Iraq. US influence in Romania has come at the expense of France, which initially championed Romania's entry into NATO and the EU. Poland's role as the key US ally in continental Europe has been strengthened by the victory of the populist Kaczynski government and close Polish-US cooperation over energy security, as well as by growing fears of Russia.

In conjunction with the policy of reformulating the NATO mandate to include out-of-area actions, the United States has begun to transform its military posture by shifting troops and resources from western Europe—and especially Germany—to the "arc of instability" linking the Black Sea region to the Middle East. Even as France, Germany, and Russia sought to prevent the US invasion of Iraq in the spring of 2003, Romania and Bulgaria publicly stated their willingness to cooperate strategically with the United States. Both countries provided access to their military bases and eventually sent substantial numbers of troops to Iraq. In November 2005, Romania and the United States agreed to the installation of US military bases at Kogalniceanu Airport, near the Black Sea port of Costanta, and Fetesti, 200 miles east of Bucharest, with the provision that US warships would patrol in the Black Sea. Romanian military analyst Cornel Codita observed that the agreement "allows the United States to move closer to Russia and above all to hot spots in the Middle East" (Codita, 2005: p. 1). Similar agreements were made with Bulgaria for the establishment of a base near Bezmer Airfield, near the southern border with Turkey (Bordonaro, 2005b). In 2007 Poland and the Czech Republic declared their intention to deploy US antiballistic missiles on their territory. These agreements, signed in the teeth of popular outcry throughout Europe over revelations of CIA prisons and overflights in Europe, signal the formation of strategic alliances between Atlanticist blocs in "new Europe" and the United States, rather than support for an autonomous regional security identity. They will be consummated by extensive economic and military-industrial linkages to the United States.[5]

Limits of European Security and Defense Policy

The CFSP originated in the late 1980s in the context of a Franco–West German project that recognized the need for an integral relationship between monetary and political union. However, the vague language concerning CFSP in the Maastricht Treaty reflected both traditional British concerns for the primacy of the transatlantic relationship and the sharp conflicts of interest that developed over German reunification and the wars in the former Yugoslavia. France has traditionally viewed a common European foreign policy as a means of countering US power, whereas, throughout the 1990s, Britain and Germany insisted any defense identity should be within the NATO framework. The Balkan wars, especially the 1999 war with Serbia, demonstrated European dependence resulting from the gap between European and US military capabilities and prompted a renewed commitment to an ESDP. At the end of 2005, the EU, whose member states combined would constitute the second-largest military force in the world, was conducting seven separate operations in Africa, Iraq, the Caucasus, and southeastern Europe. Having formed a sixty-thousand-troop rapid reaction force, the EU was deploying seven thousand troops in Bosnia and had conducted more modest interventions in Darfur and the Democratic Republic of Congo. These peacekeeping or constabulary missions do not, however, signify the development of genuine European global military capabilities or autonomy from the United States. ESDP has remained limited, in part as a result of Britain's traditional commitment to Atlanticism. However, even absent this commitment, the EU remains politically fragmented and unable, in the context of EMU and adverse demographic and growth rates, to develop military capacities that would enable it to approach the United States on a remotely equal scale.

Franco-German cooperation reached its rhetorical apex at the Summit of Four in April 2003, when Chirac and Schröder followed up their declaration of January 2003 (calling for joint decisionmaking) with an appeal—with Luxembourg and Belgium—for an autonomous military-planning headquarters. These initiatives were predicated on substantial political-military cooperation, but also the creation of "Franco-German industrial champions." Yet, these initiatives collapsed in the context of economic rivalries centered around German resistance to Sanofi-Synthélabo's takeover bid for Aventis, attempts to prevent Siemens from buying parts of Alstom, and the concept of "economic patriotism" (*Economist,* 2004: pp. 47–57; *Financial Times,* 2007: p. 9).

European attempts to develop significant defense-industry collaboration have nevertheless been partially successful and will be further encouraged by the formation of the European Defense Agency. By 2006, four European firms—BAE Systems, EADS, Thales, and Finmeccanica—were among the top ten global armaments firms. Concentration in the European industry was a response to the consolidation of the US defense industry around three large firms, Lockheed Martin, Boeing, and Raytheon, and fears that "European industry could be reduced to the status of sub-supplier to prime US contractors, while the key know-how is reserved for US firms" (European Commission, 2003a: p. 11). As the CEOs of BAE Systems, EADS, and Thales declared in 2004,

> Industry in Europe is under enormous competitive pressure from the United States. With U.S. defense R and D investment running at around eight times that of Europe's fragmented total, and with substantial growth in the PentaXgon's vast procurement budget in a heavily protected national market, American industries are reaching new heights. (Jones and Larrabee, 2005/2006: p. 63)

Yet, despite these collaborative efforts, European defense capabilities are continuing to fall further behind the United States. The real military capability of the EU is estimated to be 10 percent of the United States' (European Commission, 2003a: p. 5). A relatively high percentage of European defense budgets is devoted to personnel costs, but only 3 to 4 percent of European soldiers can be deployed. The European military-industrial complex remains fragmented and technologically backward, and there is no single market for defense procurement. Because of the vast discrepancy between US and European defense budgets, European defense firms are becoming more heavily dependent on the highly restricted US market. BAE Systems, Britain's largest defense contractor, is the seventh-largest US defense contractor and is widely expected to become a US firm (*Economist,* 2006b: pp. 66–67). Further access appears to depend on cooperation with US firms, which prevents these European firms from cutting the Atlantic umbilical cord. For example, the EU's attempts to develop a strategic relationship with China have been blocked by US opposition to the lifting of the EU's arms embargo and by European firms' unwillingness to jeopardize limited access to the US market. Added to these factors, the fiscal and monetary constraints of EMU preclude substantial increases in defense spending. While Britain and France have implemented modest increases in their defense budgets, German military spending has decreased substantially in real terms during the past decade (Center for Strategic and International Studies, 2005: p. 21). The US military budget is larger than the combined military budgets of the rest of the world.

These considerations provide the context for understanding US governmental and military support for a more closely integrated European defense policy and substantial increases in defense spending, as well as for the European constitutional treaty (*EUobserver,* 2005). With great clarity, Zbigniew Brzezinski (1997a) has summarized the logic of a strong Europe subordinated to the United States:

> Europe is America's essential geopolitical bridgehead in Eurasia. . . . Unlike America's links with Japan, NATO entrenches American political and military power on the Eurasian mainland. With the allied European nations still highly dependent on U.S. protection, any expansion of Europe's political scope is automatically an extension of U.S. influence. Conversely, the United States' ability to project power and influence in Eurasia relies on close transatlantic ties. (p. 75)[6]

Despite its tendency to indulge in anti-European and anti-French rhetoric, the Bush II administration has strongly supported EU defense integration in order to facilitate common US-EU operations under US leadership (Center for Strategic and International Studies, 2005). Just as concerns over EMU diminished as it became clear that the euro did not constitute a serious short- or medium-term rival to the dollar (see Chapter 2), so stronger European defense is viewed as a means of consolidating Atlanticism and expanding the US imperium. The 2006 *Quadrennial*

Defense Review anticipates a "long war" implying "long-duration, complex operations involving the US military and international partners, waged simultaneously in multiple countries round the world" (US Department of Defense, 2006: pp. 7, 13). European countries are assigned a central supporting role in this transformational strategy whose template is the NATO-led "Operation Enduring Freedom" in Afghanistan.

Europe, the United States, and the "Long War"

The contrast between the EU's apparently strong bargaining position in international trade and its geopolitical weakness has given rise to the concept of "civilian power." By proclaiming the limited utility of military force and the advantages of "soft power" in the contemporary era, proponents of this concept seek to rescue the thesis of a European challenge to US hegemony. Yet, the concept of civilian power makes an artificial and therefore misleading distinction between economic and political-military power. The dual-track enlargements of NATO and the EU have entrenched the position of political elites and transnational business interests across Europe, linked to the United States and to neoliberalism. Indeed, even if one grants the limited utility arising from the concept of soft power, the bargaining position that might, in principle, derive from the sheer weight of the European economy is compromised by the neoliberal context in which a (self-limiting) socioeconomic project demands adherence to Washington and Wall Street. Europe's geopolitical predicament thus precludes attempts to establish an autonomous EU power and marginalizes forces in "core Europe" that favor alternatives to US-led neoliberalism. Because it precludes a social democratic pact, neoliberalism has required effective restrictions of democracy, which have been accomplished by institutionalizing market-driven reforms and fiscal pacts at the level of the EU.

It is possible to conceptualize the contemporary exercise of US power in terms of "domination without hegemony" (Guha, 1992: pp. 231–232; Arrighi, 2005a: p. 32). Although this formulation is useful in capturing the increasingly parasitic and coercive aspects of US financial and military power, it does not take into account the degree of consensus and common interest among transatlantic elites that is conveyed by the concept of minimal hegemony. As already discussed, the leading sectors of European business have acquiesced to the new economic and security framework and derive substantial benefits from it, even as their societies experience low growth and high unemployment. For example, German industry pursues a highly profitable export-led growth strategy, heavily dependent on outsourcing in Eastern Europe and capital outflows to the United States. In 2005, the stock market rose by 25 percent in Germany, 23 percent in France, 16 percent in the UK, and 13 percent in Italy (Thornhill, 2005: p. 9).[7] Monetary and fiscal policies in Europe do not derive from monetarist dogma alone, but more fundamentally from the concrete interests of powerful actors responding to the constraints and incentives of a given transatlantic regulatory order.

Terminal Crisis?

There are nevertheless clear signs that even this more tenuous and unstable type of leadership—what we have called "minimal hegemony"—may be eroding. A brutal and costly occupation of Iraq has once again raised the specter of geopolitical overstretch, antagonizing world public opinion and tarnishing the domestic ideological legitimacy of the Bush administration. The extraordinary intervention of the Iraq Study Group has thrown a spotlight on factional divisions, which appear to be sharpening as the occupation founders. The costs of the occupation have been defrayed by fiscal deficits that have deepened the United States' dependency on foreign capital. Can US hegemony recover from the Iraqi quagmire, resolve its financial problems, and reconsolidate its position as the leader of a capitalist core? Giovanni Arrighi (2005a) asserts that the United States stands at the precipice of a "terminal crisis," resulting from geopolitical overstretch and financial insolvency, that is leading to confrontation with China:

> Far from laying the foundations of a second American Century, the occupation of Iraq has jeopardized the credibility of U.S. military might, further undermined the centrality of the United States and its currency within the global political economy, and strengthened the tendency towards the emergence of China as an alternative to U.S. leadership in East Asia and beyond. (p. 80)

He argues that the crisis presents Europe with a variety of options, including the establishment of closer ties with China or the recasting of the Atlantic order, based on Keynesian and social-democratic precepts (see also Harvey, 2003; Reid, 2004; Hutton, 2002; Wallerstein, 2003).

As Chapter 2 shows, the ability of the United States to attract massive capital inflows has served as the linchpin of the minimally hegemonic order. Yet, the continuation of these inflows has been called into question by growing US trade and budget deficits. To be sure, a precipitous decline in the value of the dollar would make it more difficult to sustain large US military expenditures and would contest a concept of economic governance based on consumer debt. In 2004, total securities invested in the United States amounted to $33.4 trillion, or 50 percent of the world total. The 2006 US current account deficit reached $869 billion, or 6.6 percent of national income; the trade deficit with China was $202 billion. In 2006, the US budget deficit was $248 billion, or 2.3 percent of GDP, representing a substantial decline in relation to 2005 (United States Treasury, 2006). Chinese dollar reserves totaled nearly $800 billion at the end of 2005 and were expected to surpass $1,000 billion in 2006 (*Financial Times,* 2006b: p. 1). Whereas, until the turn of the twenty-first century capital inflows were largely private equity funds in the form of foreign direct investment or portfolio investment, during the first years of the new century the composition of these inflows has changed significantly. They are now coming primarily from governments or institutions representing governments (Feldstein, 2006: p. 15). Hence, there is both a political and a market logic to capital inflows. The strength of the dollar once again depends in part on explicit or implicit international pacts, as it did during the mid- and late 1960s.

As the size of the budget and trade deficits increases, US fiscal and monetary autonomy increasingly depends on the willingness of foreign governments to continue to purchase and hold dollars. Despite widespread expectations of eventual dollar devaluation, Asian investors and governments have, in fact, continued to increase their dollar holdings, because most of their trade is with the United States and because they maintain undervalued exchange rates in order to continue export-led growth and employment strategies that render them highly dependent on access to the US market. China runs substantial trade deficits with its East Asian trading partners; hence, all East Asian economies, and not simply China's, have a high degree of vulnerability to any decrease in US demand.

The potential dangers of the US deficits and the impact of a low savings rate and an overvalued dollar on US manufacturing are, of course, widely recognized. The size of the budget deficit has grown due to large increases in spending on the military and homeland security, large supplemental expenditures to fund the Iraq occupation, and the Bush tax cuts. Moreover, even if the United States can continue to attract sizeable capital inflows, the size of the budget deficit may reduce the ability of the Federal Reserve Board to continue to stimulate demand and respond aggressively to such emergencies as the September 11 terrorist attacks (Weisberg, 2006: p. 15). Notwithstanding mutual dependency between US and foreign central banks, there is broad agreement that the dollar will continue to depreciate in the coming years, although the pace and extent of depreciation are unpredictable. There is also speculation that China, which has gradually permitted modest appreciations of the renminbi, will continue to diversify its foreign exchange reserves away from the US dollar and government bonds. Arrighi (2005a) concludes:

> In reality the sinking dollar of the 2000s is the expression of a far more serious crisis of American hegemony than the sinking dollar of the 1970s. Whether gradual or brutal, it is the expression (and a factor) of a relative and absolute loss of the US's capacity to retain its centrality within the global political economy. (p. 74)

A precipitous decline of the dollar would have serious and unpredictable consequences not only for the world economy, but also for US domestic politics. As Chapter 2 suggests, the neoliberal project in the United States has been predicated on high levels of consumption for the middle and upper classes, made possible in part by the privileges of dollar hegemony. US income and consumption levels would be hit hard by a combination of tax increases, dollar devaluation, and rising interest rates (Duménil and Lévy, 2004). Moreover, the inability of the United States to secure significant levels of direct financial support for military intervention, as it did during the first Gulf War, implies a closer relationship between its financial problems and its overall military posture. The difficulties of the Iraqi occupation have encouraged Iranian intransigence and emboldened challengers to US hegemony in Latin America. China has made significant political and economic incursions into the Middle East and Africa, and has signed long-term oil contracts with Saudi Arabia, Iran, and Libya. The calculated provocations of the Bush administration, typified by the 2002 declaration of the right to wage preemptive wars unilaterally, have produced fear but also resistance. The conduct of the war on terror and of the Iraqi occupation have further weakened US credibility and standing throughout the world.

New US Century?

The manifold economic and political uncertainties of the present period of international relations—marked, above all, by the extreme volatility of the Persian Gulf region—render all predictions about the future trajectory of US hegemony hazardous. Yet, if the war in Iraq and growing financial problems have clearly blown the United States into uncharted waters, it is not yet clear that US hegemony has entered a terminal phase; even less predictable is the nature of a putative endgame and its impact on Europe.

The significance of data on the US current account deficit and capital inflows depends on assumptions about the long-term political and economic strategies of states and investors. As we note in Chapter 2, the United States was, until 1989 (and Britain prior to 1914), a net creditor; however, since 1971 US hegemony has depended more on its central position in global capital markets than on industrial strength or capital outflows.[8] It is almost certain that foreign liabilities will gradually diminish with future dollar depreciations (or Asian revaluations), as they did in 2002 and 2003. More importantly, the import bias that accounts for these liabilities reflects in part the dominance of US multinational corporations in world trade, as well as the relatively high growth and productivity rates of the US economy in relation to Japan and Europe. Sales of US foreign affiliates are three times as great as US exports. Approximately 20 percent of US imports from China are from US multinationals. MNC investment abroad adds to the US current-account deficit. An ownership-based concept of trade would reduce the current-account deficit by at least 25 percent (Farrell, 2005: p. 13). The hegemonic position of US capital is in no sense territorially based; 700 military facilities located outside the US "homeland" in 130 countries represent the projection abroad of US state power to protect the interests of a global economic imperium.

Asian (and to some extent European) investors and governments have extraordinarily strong incentives to continue to finance US imports in order to maintain their export-led growth strategies. There are substantial complementarities between the Asian growth strategies and the US economy. As Levey and Brown write, "Only a fundamental transformation in Asia's growth strategy could undermine this mutually advantageous interdependence" (2005: p. 4). With respect to China, the possibilities for such a transformation need to be assessed within the context of the massive and violent absorption of two hundred million peasants into urban areas—with all of the attendant political dangers and uncertainties that this process entails—and a highly unstable banking sector. The combination of low growth and the structural problems of the eurozone, as discussed in Chapters 2 and 3, make it highly unlikely that the euro could challenge the key currency role of the dollar, especially given the impact of a depreciating dollar on European growth rates. Although it is possible, as Arrighi suggests (2005a: pp. 73–74), that the dollar might give way to a multiple reserve currency system, the international political economy has never experienced a stable, enduring system of multiple currencies. There is a great deal of evidence that international monetary stability requires hegemonic leadership (Kindleberger, 1973). In this respect, although the United States no longer serves as a net creditor and despite its extractive financial posture, it nevertheless continues to provide significant "public goods," including those of buyer of last resort, technology transfer, and monetary anchor. As the concept of minimal hegemony implies, these public goods relate to a narrower social base than during the "golden age."

To be sure, the costs of the war and occupation of Iraq have vastly exceeded the wildly optimistic initial projections of the Bush administration. According to the administration's own figures, the cost stood at $173 billion at the end of 2005. Independent sources suggest the real costs would be in the range of $1 billion to $2 billion by the end of 2006 (Bilmes and Stiglitz, 2006). The US military budget has increased substantially since 2001; it exceeded $500 billion in 2006. Yet, the significance of this spending needs to be assessed within the context of a growth model that is highly dependent on the military-industrial complex. At less than 5 percent of GDP, US spending on the military and foreign policy is a percentage point less than during the Reagan build-up of the 1980s, and less than half the Cold War level of the 1950s. Military Keynesianism has been a fundamental characteristic of the US economy and the political spoils system. The militarization of foreign policy has undoubtedly served to increase growth rates and buttress the economic and political-electoral base of the Republican right, especially in the US South. These factors caution against the assumption that, for purely economic reasons, the United States will be unable to continue to finance significant forward military deployments and, where necessary, undertake military intervention.[9]

Control of global petroleum reserves has been central to the exercise of US hegemony since 1945. Strategic primacy in the Middle East—just as in Central Asia—has become increasingly important to the United States at a time of declining oil supply. Hence the invasion of Iraq represents one part of the more general project of the United States designed to assert geopolitical primacy in Eurasia and maintain US hegemony in the face of challenges from Russia, China, Japan, and Europe (Harvey, 2003). The Iranian Revolution of 1979 signified an important setback for the United States in the Middle East. During the 1980s, the United States was compelled to pursue a defensive policy of dual containment of Iraq and Iran, designed to prevent the emergence of a single regional power.

However, the collapse of the Soviet Union provided opportunities for the United States (with British support) to reassert its primacy in the region. Prior to 2003, the United States' unwillingness to commit large numbers of troops to the Middle East led it to seek, through sanctions, to keep Iraqi oil off the world market and prevent Iraq from developing commercial relations with rivals. By the late 1990s, when the United States initiated large-scale air attacks against Iraq, this strategy had begun to break down. Moreover, the September 11 terrorist attacks showed that further challenges to US authority were arising in Saudi Arabia. The invasion and subsequent occupation of Iraq thus represented an attempt to devise a military solution to these problems. As Michael Klare (2006) has written,

> The war against Iraq was intended to provide the United States with a dominant position in the Persian Gulf region, and to serve as a springboard for further conquests and assertion of power in the region. . . . It is part of a larger process of asserting dominant U.S. power in south-central Asia, in the very heartland of this mega-continent. (p. 10)

The strength of the Iraqi resistance, the intensity of the civil war, and the sheer ineptitude of the Bush administration have, to say the least, greatly increased the costs and difficulties of this project. At the same time, however, the United States has not relinquished its goal of re-asserting its control over Iraqi oil and fortifying a network of permanent military bases throughout the country.

The United States has begun to implement a "revolutionary grand design in Asia" (Twining, 2006: p. 15), with a view to containing China, which it has designated as its chief "strategic competitor." Since 2001, Japan has made a historic decision to close ranks with the United States against China; the United States has also deepened ties with Australia and South Korea, which will be solidified through the development of an anti-ballistic missile system (Bordonaro, 2006b: p. 2). The hypernationalist and neoliberal Koizumi government (2001–2006) adopted an extremely provocative stance toward China, including security guarantees with Taiwan, Singapore, and India; developing additional naval power, including light aircraft carriers; undertaking joint military exercises with the United States; and sending troops to Iraq (McCormack, 2005; Baker, 2006: p. 3). Japan has also launched extensive diplomatic and economic initiatives in Central Asia, designed to counteract the influence of the Shanghai Cooperation Organization (Len, 2006). In October 2005, the United States and Japan jointly declared their intention "to develop options and adapt the alliance to the changing regional and global security environment" (Ministry of Foreign Affairs of Japan, 2005). China and Japan have deployed combat planes and ships against each other in disputed areas of the East China Sea with deposits of natural gas.

The United States has also entered into a de facto alliance with India, which it considers a "great power and key strategic partner" (United States Department of Defense, 2006a: p. 40), based on US support for India's nuclear weapons program, India's decision to vote with the United States in the International Atomic Energy Agency to refer Iran to the Security Council, India's participation in the US-sponsored Turkmenistan-Afghanistan-Pakistan (TAP) natural gas pipeline, and the complementarities between India's neoliberal reforms and the US service economy (Pant, 2006; *Asia Times,* 2006: p. 1).[10] The significance of the Asian "grand design" cannot be overestimated, especially in conjunction with US advances in Eastern Europe and Central Asia. Despite (very limited) understandings between Russia and China, there has been no significant "balancing" against the United States at the global level, and no competitor has yet achieved regional hegemony.

Theorists of hegemonic decline, finally, have laid considerable stress on US domestic opposition to the Iraq War and subsequent occupation. Philip Golub, for example, has cited "growing disarray at home" and a "deep and growing fracture within US institutions over the neoimperialist agenda of the new right" (2004: p. 780). Yet, tactical differences between "realists" committed to consensual hegemonic practices and "neoconservatives" committed to aggressive unilateralism must be understood within a broader context of strategic agreement and essential continuity between the Clinton and Bush administrations. The Iraq Study Group called only for "strategic redeployment" and a gradual reduction of ground troops in Iraq. The National Security Advisory Group, the leading Democratic Party voice on foreign policy, has appealed for the expansion of the US military by thirty thousand troops and a commander-in-chief "who can inspire a nation of young people to serve" (National Security Advisory Group, 2006: pp. 17, 21–22). Notwithstanding its ties to neoconservatives, since 2004 the Bush White House, Treasury, and State Department have forged increasingly close links to Wall Street (Kirchgaessner and White, 2006: p. 3).[11]

Although popular opposition to the occupation of Iraq has increased greatly since 2003, it seems doubtful that US society is capable at the present time of summoning the radical impulses necessary to challenge a broader imperial project that enjoys the support of a unified elite. By linking Iraq to the terrorist attacks of September 11, the Bush administration gave itself a virtual blank check for military intervention in the Middle

East. If domestic opposition to the war in Iraq has grown, it is less clear that the more general state of emergency and permanent mobilization—"the long war"—is abating.[12] In what Anatol Lieven (2004: p. 88) calls "the embittered heartland," communities have been hollowed out and traumatized by deindustrialization, the collapse of trade unions, and an ethic of the marketplace. In this soil, a particularly virulent strain of militant US nationalism has been cultivated and conjoined with Christian fundamentalism.

In this respect at least, the United States and Europe resemble each other. Neoliberal Europe confronts the crisis of legitimation, with its own mutually reinforcing combination of market rationality and resurgent nationalism. Whereas US nationalism has been harnessed to an expansive and aggressive imperial project, nationalism in Europe is socially implosive and parochial, but not without its own dangers. The end of the Cold War has not led to greater European autonomy and self-determination. Rather, it has reinforced adherence to a market-driven integration project that is radically at odds with its traditions and ideals, and subordinated to a US imperium that, notwithstanding its fragility, continues to cast a very wide shadow.

Notes

1. The Constitutional Treaty for Europe stipulated that "[t]he policy of the union" must be "compatible" with NATO (Article I-4-2). Policies should be "consistent with commitments under NATO, which for those states that are members of it, remains the foundation of their collective defense and the forum for its implementation" (I-41-7).

2. West German Chancellor Genscher declared, "What NATO must do is state unequivocally that whatever happens in the Warsaw Pact there will be no expansion of NATO territory eastwards, that is to say closer to the borders of the Soviet Union" (Zelikow and Rice, 1995: p. 182). Notably, as early as November 1992, Secretary of Defense Cheney declared, "I, for one, would advocate that eventually we will want to expand NATO and move it to the East" (Goldgeier, 1999: p. 18).

3. In September 2000, the Albanian-Macedonian-Bulgarian Oil Pipeline Corporation (AMBO), an Anglo-US firm based in New York City, signed a memorandum of understanding with the three countries for exclusive rights to a project for a 900-kilometer pipeline from Burgas (Bulgaria) to Vlore (Albania). The projected pipeline runs adjacent to the Presevo Valley and Camp Bondsteel. A second US military base, Camp Monteith, is located in Gnjilane, 60 kilometers to the north (GlobalSecurity.org, 2006; Trofimov, 2003; *Financial Times,* 2005c: p. 4).

4. In 78 days of air strikes, NATO forces flew 32,000 sorties and dropped 21,000 tons of bombs on Serbia, Montenegro, and Kosovo. Estimates of civilian casualties run from 1,000 to 2,000 killed and 3,000 to 6,000 injured. NATO forces did not have a single casualty (Cafruny, 2003).

5. The US Committee on NATO, the leading lobby for the expansion of NATO in Central and Eastern Europe, was founded in 1994 by Lockheed Martin vice president Bruce Jackson. Lockheed Martin's $3.5 billion contract with Poland for the F-16 fighter, signed at the end of 2002, cemented close US-Polish relations and served as a template for further US defense industry involvement in the "new Europe" (*Guardian,* 2002). Jackson, a charter member of the Project for the New American Century, has worked closely with pro-US lobbies in Romania, Bulgaria, Georgia, and Ukraine and recently has championed the goal of breaking Gazprom's monopoly on supply and transit of natural gas to Europe, through the construction of an alternate southern transit route from the Caspian to Europe (Jackson, 2006: pp. 9–11). When Romanian president Basescu visited Washington in March 2005, Jackson stated that "the Black Sea is already vital for European energy acquisition, and that it will be even more so in the future" (Bordonaro, 2005a: p. 3).

6. Or, as Brzezinski reiterated in 2004, "An essentially multilateralist Europe and a somewhat unilateralist America make for a perfect global marriage of convenience. . . . Neither America nor Europe could do as well without the other. Together, they are the core of global stability" (p. 96).

7. In February 2006, Volkswagen announced plans to cut 20,000 jobs over the next three years, one-fifth of the west German workforce, even as operating profits for 2005 were up by 70 percent (*Financial Times,* 2006a: p. 1).

8. US share of GDP, in contrast to Britain, has remained relatively steady at around 20 percent, although its composition has become more heavily weighted in services.

9. "The annual war bill represents only about one cent of the $12 trillion of national income each year, and the total military cost at most, a nickel. . . . [T]he foundation of U.S. international influence is its large, powerful economy which can absorb the narrow, resource costs of war and free the U.S. to pursue strategic and security goals" (Holtz-Eakin, 2006: p. 15).

10. The United States and France have also cooperated closely outside of Europe. France helped to engineer the coup d'état against Haitian president Aristide in 2004 and assisted in the "Cedar Revolution," leading to the removal of Syrian troops from Lebanon.

11. The assumption of a "neoconservative imperial project" (see also Arrighi, 2005a: p. 74) overlooks this essential unity. The backgrounds of the key architects of the Iraq war and of the Bush National Security Strategy of 2002 reinforce this point. Richard Cheney: Council on Foreign Relations (CFR), Business Council; Colin Powell: CFR; Condoleezza Rice: CFR; Donald Rumsfeld: Trilateral Commission, Salomon Smith Barney; Bilderburg: World Economic Forum, Bretton Woods Committee; Paul Wolfowitz: Trilateral Commission; L. Paul Bremer: Council on Foreign Relations, Kissinger Associates. Lawrence Wilkerson, Colin Powell's chief of staff from 2001 to 2005 and widely regarded for his criticism of an alleged "neoconservative cabal," has stated that US troops will need to remain in Iraq for between five and eight

years, because "it is strategic in the sense that Vietnam was not." Likewise, a precipitous withdrawal "without leaving something behind we can trust, we will mobilize the nation, with five million men and women under arms to go back and take the Middle East within a decade" (Interpress Service, 2005).

Both of the leading 2008 Democratic presidential candidates, Hillary Clinton and Barack Obama, are proponents of a highly militarized and interventionist US foreign policy. According to the Democratic Leadership Council, in which Hillary Clinton plays a leading role,

> America needs a bigger and better military . . . the escalating conflicts in Iraq and Afghanistan have stretched the all-volunteer force to the breaking point. Democrats should step forward with a plan to repair the damage, by adding more troops, replenishing depleted stocks of equipment, and reorganizing the force around the new missions of unconventional warfare, counterinsurgency, and civil reconstruction. (Democratic Leadership Council, 2006)

Obama has called for an expansion of US ground forces by 65,000 and of marines by 27,000; large increases of US and NATO troops in Afghanistan; and a continuing US military presence in Iraq including an "over the horizon force that could prevent chaos in the wider [Middle East] region" (Obama '08, 2007: p. 1).

12. According to a Zogby International poll (February 2006), 47 percent of Americans favored military action to stop Iran's nuclear program, which the Bush administration has acknowledged is ten years from completion; 27 percent cited Iran as the "greatest menace" to Washington, up from 9 percent four months previously (Interpress Service, 2006: p. 1).

6

Conclusion

WHAT WE HAVE CALLED EUROPE'S "second project of integration" was a result in part of ideological and institutional factors that have been explored at considerable length in the literature on the EU. Yet, ideas and institutions have not in themselves been the decisive or most salient factors in establishing the particular socioeconomic content that the EU has acquired since the mid-1980s. By creating a customs union and a common agricultural policy, the Treaty of Rome served as an adjunct to the social- and Christian-democratic–inspired social accords between capital and labor that developed after World War II. By helping to cement these accords, the first project contributed to the material basis of social citizenship and thereby served to stabilize and integrate national societies. The second project, beginning with the SEA and culminating in the EMU and the attendant Lisbon and Cardiff processes, represented a fundamental departure from the norms and practices of the EU through its first three decades. This project has served as the key vehicle through which social pacts and national regulatory systems are being retrenched. To be sure, in some important respects—most notably EMU—the result has been an "ever closer union." Yet, at the same time, the neoliberal features of the second project have generated powerful disintegrative effects within member states as well as within the EU as a whole.

The design of the EMU is inherently connected to the US-dominated transnational order. Europe's subordinate position within this order preempts the possibility of resolving structural problems of postindustrial—or, as we prefer, post-Fordist—society in a manner consistent with Europe's distinctive social accords. Economic stagnation, uneven development, and the widening gap between new forms of economic governance and social citizenship amplify legitimation problems and political conflicts, with adverse effects on the EU's political ability to mobilize a political counterweight to the United States.

Although we have focused in this book on the fundamental changes that have taken place in the structure of advanced capitalist societies and in the norms and institutions that have governed relations among them since 1945, we have also drawn attention to important continuities in transatlantic power relations. The Maastricht Treaty and the end of the Cold War did not give rise to a more independent Europe. Just as the Treaty of Rome established a framework of European economic cooperation—Europe's first project of integration—that accorded with the US *integral* hegemony of the Bretton Woods system, so has the project of single market and monetary union been undertaken as a result of Europe's subordination to the American imperium, albeit one that has become more precarious, or minimally hegemonic.

An emphasis on *structural power,* we argue, provides a more satisfactory analytical framework for characterizing the nature and scope of transatlantic power relations than a *basic-force* model, which defines power in terms of a given state's relative possession of resources. In its classical formulation, the basic-force model was measured in terms of national output in such basic industries as steel and coal (Lenin, 1916) or aggregate national economic output (Organski and Kugler, 1981). As the industrial infrastructure of the United States' post–World War II leadership began to erode in the late 1960s and early 1970s, international relations scholars revived this model to support their predictions of US hegemonic decline (Gilpin, 1973; Keohane, 1980). The history of the past three decades has not been kind to these predictions, but successive analyses deploying variants of the basic-force model have merely pushed the time of decline into the future, each suggesting that "this time" the end is really in sight.

The proposition of an emergent European economic superpower is based on a basic-force model. It asserts that the EU has reached a position of global economic leadership by virtue of its equality with the United States in terms of GDP and presence in world trade. In order for this proposition to be compelling, two corollary assumptions are required: first, for economic purposes, the EU can be viewed as a polity or at least a single actor; and, second, in the contemporary era of globalization, military power has lost much of its utility, not least because it has become decoupled from economic power. Joseph Nye, for example, acknowledges the persistence and relevance of US military hegemony, but argues that it has become less salient. He asserts that the world is "multipolar" with respect to "interstate economic issues," such that the concept of hegemony no longer makes sense, and that "power is widely distributed and chaotically organized among state and non-state actors" with respect to transnational economic issues (2002: p. 1). Therefore, European power consists of cultural influence, "including that of its own process of unification" (2003: p. 1; see also Nye, 2004). Pursuing this line of thought, John McCormick contends that "Europeanism emphasizes the post-modern values of peace, multilateralism, internationalism, soft power, and civilian means for dealing with conflict" (2007: p. 167).

In fact, the basic-force model greatly overstates the nature and extent of the decline of US hegemony. It fails to account for the ways in which Washington and Wall Street were able successfully to reconfigure US hegemony after the collapse of the Bretton Woods system on the basis of the interactive embeddedness of public, corporate, and retail financial and money markets in accordance with US welfare residualism. By contrast, the Maastricht design of EMU, fiscal pacts, and the Lisbon reform process have not established an adequate foundation for sustained European economic growth and political cohesion. Rather, they have introduced selectively within the EU—and especially within the eurozone—institutions and practices that are incompatible with European systems of innovation and social accords and that reinforce US-led neoliberal hegemony. The result has been chronic uneven development, stagnation, and unemployment. These factors, in turn, fan the flames of nationalist populism and prevent the emergence of a genuine polity and the mobilization of a coherent EU foreign policy agency.

Those who have made their way through the preceding chapters will also be in no doubt that we are sceptical of claims that international economic relations are multipolar or chaotically organized, or that globalization has decoupled military power from international and transnational economic relations. More broadly, the distinction between political and economic power implicit in basic-force and soft-power models is analytical, and not real. Since 1945, US hegemony in Europe has been expressed through the mutual interaction of political military and economic power. The United States' geopolitical expansion across the European continent after 1989 was itself a key factor in the consolidation of neoliberalism. Indeed, China's rapid ascendance, the resurgence of Russian nationalism, growing instability in the Middle East, and the resource rivalries that are likely to become increasingly acute in the coming decades throw a spotlight on the continuing realities of geopolitical rivalry and the limitations of Europe's nascent security project.

Speculation in the United States about a rising European superpower is perhaps not surprising. It is simultaneously a reflection of the dreams of a marginalized left and the nightmares of a fearful right in an era of great intellectual turmoil and ambiguity. The future trajectory of US power is uncertain. The precariousness of US minimal hegemony, resulting from the accelerating pace of US industrial decline and growing US reliance on torrential inflows of capital from Asia and Europe, has been exacerbated by dangerous and self-destructive policies of the neoconservatives of the Bush administration, not least in the Middle East.

For the American right, the launch of the euro and the unprecedented Franco-German attempt to prevent the US invasion of Iraq breathed new life into its perennial fears of European challenge, even if more astute observers understood its limitations (e.g., Kagan, 2003; Center for Strategic and International Studies, 2005). Across the political spectrum, US liberals, disillusioned British Labourites, and "third way" social democrats were naturally attracted to Europe's distinctive commitments to the social market, cosmopolitan human rights norms, and multilateralism (see especially Hutton, 2002; Reid, 2004; McCormick, 2007). Strongly opposed to the frankly imperialist attitudes and policies of the Bush administration, overwhelming majorities on the European continent, and even an increasing number of people in the United States, anticipated this challenge hopefully (BBC World Service, 2007). Amid massive protests throughout Europe in the spring of 2003, Jürgen Habermas, Jacques Derrida, and other leading intellectuals proclaimed the "birth of a European public" that might "bring its full weight to bear at the international level and within the United Nations in order to balance the hegemonic unilateralism of the United States" (Derrida and Habermas, 2003: p. 33).

Yet, even if it is possible to identify a set of distinctive European values in the arena of world politics—a Kantian ethic that stands in opposition to an increasingly militarized US foreign policy—the fruits of this ethic have been rather meager. To be sure, the list of global operations in which the EU participates continues to grow. Yet, one searches in vain for areas of substantive involvement where European countries either individually or collectively have carried out sustained programs of crisis management or peacekeeping in the absence of support and patronage from the American superpower (much less in opposition to it) and in ways that run contrary to demonstrable European geopolitical and economic interests. Even amid crushing setbacks in the Middle East, the United States has begun to construct a new network of strategic alliances well beyond the European sphere, predicated on close Anglo-US collaboration, but into which NATO forces are likely to become integrated.

Europe's impotence with respect to the invasion and occupation of Iraq repeated the experiences of Bosnia and Kosovo; the rhetoric of "European identity" and opposition to the United States could not overcome the force of the transatlantic neoliberal alliance and the vagaries and opportunism of Franco-German cooperation (Deppe, 2004: pp. 320–321). Despite torrents of rhetoric condemning the invasion plans, the EU provided substantial logistical support to the Iraqi invasion, while, in its aftermath, France and Germany adopted a pro-Washington stance on virtually all significant global questions. With respect to issues of global economic governance, moreover, the EU has thrown full support behind neoliberal policies of structural adjustment, trade liberalization, and agricultural protectionism. French-led attempts to abandon the embargo on arms sales to China in support of a broader commercial offensive were quietly abandoned when confronted by Washington's opposition.

Nor has the EU engaged in sustained efforts to use its soft power to promote human rights outside of its own domain. As Kenneth Roth has written, "As a collection of democracies founded on respect for the rule of law and the rights of the individual, the EU should be a natural human rights leader. It has performed impressively in extending these values to its new members and occasionally elsewhere, but when acting beyond its borders the EU is often disappointingly weak" (2007: p. 11). To point out the inability of the EU to project its self-declared values under the terms of its present construction is in no sense to diminish either its significant historical accomplishments nor to suggest that a stronger and more unified EU is not, in principle, a desirable objective. Europe's contemporary role as an *object,* and not a *subject,* in international affairs is not ultimately a result of institutional shortcomings or a lack of political will, although these problems surely exist. Rather, it is a function of the political and economic weaknesses that result from subordination to US-led neoliberalism.

Our emphasis on EMU as the institutional fulcrum of Europe's second project implies that the economic policies that are directly or indirectly carried out at the supranational level are playing a central role in the political economy of the member states, both individually and collectively. This claim, axiomatic to some segments of the European left, and indeed widely recognized by most economists, is not universally held. In his analysis of the referendum on the Constitutional Treaty, Andrew Moravcsik, for example, contends that "nearly all the most salient issues in the minds of European voters—fiscal priorities, social policy and health care, pensions, education, infrastructure, and such—remain national" (2006b: p. 226). Therefore, "wholesale constitutional reform had little legal or substantive justification" (p. 219). Indeed, opposition to the treaty in the Netherlands and France has little significance for European politics because it was based on ignorance, apathy, and symbolic protest (p. 227). According to Moravcsik, no further constitutional efforts at legitimation are necessary or desirable precisely because "the issues the EU deals with most intensely . . . are not salient issues for the mass public. The most salient issues, notably those involving fiscal outlays, remain firmly national" (p. 225). Indeed, the failure of the treaty is evidence that the "*gran projet,*" as Moravcsik calls it, of the single market and monetary union has resulted in "the success and stability of the existing European constitutional settlement" (p. 219).

Such a perspective overlooks the most interesting and radical features of the contemporary EU. It fails to comprehend the extent to which the second integration project—in contrast to the first—is transforming European society and politics through imposing a logic of neoliberal restructuring. While the failure of the referenda certainly had many origins, a great deal of opposition to the treaty resulted from resistance to these reforms. This was especially the case in France, but also, to a greater extent than is usually recognized, in the Netherlands (van Apeldoorn, 2006).

Indeed, this Panglossian view of the referenda—and more broadly of EMU—is not only contrary to the views of a broad segment of the European left, but also to those of national and European governing elites who fully recognize the precariousness of the monetary union. Thus, while the defeat of the referenda gave evidence of broad resistance to neoliberalism, there is also concern within the European Commission, the ECB, the OECD, and national governments that what we have called Europe's "halfway house" of monetarism and incomplete structural reforms is incompatible with the continuation of the monetary union. The statement of the former commissioner for competition policy, Frits Bolkestein (2001), to the effect that Europe would need to abandon the comforts of the Rhineland model to achieve the Lisbon objectives, is only the most prominent and emblematic confirmation of this sentiment. This recognition drives the repeated and forceful warnings that, in the absence of genuine labor mobility, deeper and more comprehensive structural reforms will be necessary to preserve the monetary union. Yet, such reforms, even if they could overcome the opposition from labor movements and other welfare state constituencies that still retain considerable defensive strength, would exacerbate—and not resolve—the economic problems of the eurozone. Proponents of neoliberal reforms seriously underestimate the extent to which expansive and stable demand in and of itself remains a central mechanism of economic development in post-Fordist capitalism—the sort of expansion that the EMS and EMU have consistently choked off. Furthermore, the continuation of EMU in its present form is not compatible with the levels of social provision required to reproduce existing norms of social citizenship.

Does the sociopolitical impasse—in which the alleged imperatives of neoliberal austerity collide with the residual political institutions and sociocultural ethos of the postwar settlement—justify our contention of a social and political crisis? In Chapter 4, we argue that the pressures on the welfare state, emanating from EMU-driven (and previously EMS-driven) self-limitation, do indeed generate powerful disintegrative tendencies that put in question the very balance of T. H. Marshall's triptych of social, civic, and political citizenship that has produced the rather fortuitous compatibility of capitalism and democracy in post–World War II Western Europe. These disintegrative tendencies include the decline of mass parties and a concomitant decrease in the power and membership of trade unions and other civic associations; declining voter turnout; the growth of racist and anti-Muslim sentiment; and the rise of new right parties and movements and of populist mavericks. These phenomena, in turn, can be linked to a broader sense of depoliticization and drift, as aptly summarized by Peter Mair (2006),

> A sense of dispersal and atomization marks the broader organization environment in which the traditional parties used to nest. As workers' parties, or as religious parties, the mass parties in Europe rarely stood on their own, but constituted the core element within a wider and more complex network of trade unions, churches, business associations, mutual societies, and social clubs. These helped to root the old mass parties in society and to stabilize and distinguish their electorates. (p. 46)

The result has been a trend toward antipolitical sentiments, concentration of executive power, and elite demands for nondemocratic decision-making and output efficiency, not least at the level of the EU.[1] The ECB has served as the template for the "politics of antipolitics." Formal democracy remains, but regional and global governance further reduce the scope for substantive national democratic expression. Traditional understandings of citizenship are eroding as mass parties are losing their way.

The emphasis in this book on the continuities of the United States' transatlantic hegemony suggests that, in the absence of radical social and political change in Europe, external factors, such as the ways in which the United States responds to its twin financial and geopolitical crises, will have a great impact on Europe's future. Across the political spectrum, and especially on the left, there are expectations of a full-blown crisis of the dollar. Yet, ever since the collapse of the Bretton Woods system, there has been a tendency to underestimate the ability of the United States to reconstitute its primacy on both economic and political levels. Given the complexity and fluidity of contemporary geopolitics and geoeconomics, predictions are—to say the least—hazardous. Still, despite its increasingly unstable underpinnings, it is probable that the fundamental resiliency of the US economy (coupled with the desire of creditors to maintain exports) and the United States' underlying military power will underwrite the continuing primacy of the dollar. Similarly, in Chapter 5 we highlight the ways in which the Bush administration has acted on the capacities that existing structures still grant US policymakers to establish new strategic alliances intended to counter tendencies to hegemonic decline. We are not convinced that these policies—over which there is consensus well beyond doctrinaire neocon circles—are predestined to fail.

The United States' growing financial difficulties have led to a modest but significant shift from the dollar to the euro. Of course, the euro might be the beneficiary of a full-blown dollar crisis, although its credibility in foreign exchange markets has been bought at a heavy price. Yet, if predictions concerning the future of US hegemony are hazardous, it is perhaps less risky to assert that a major crisis of the dollar would not automatically lead to a corresponding shift to the euro as reserve currency and the emergence of a European economic superpower. In this sense, analogies to historical cycles in world politics are not particularly helpful. Even if the US Treasury and Wall Street were unable to avert a wholesale collapse of the dollar as a reserve currency, the result would likely be a massive downturn of the world economy, which would have an especially forceful impact on Europe's own export-led models. The degree of transatlantic economic interdependence has increased dramatically in recent years. Europe's economic growth remains closely linked to the fortunes of the US economy. This is especially the case for Germany.

What would it take, though, for Europe to translate its undoubted economic resources, critical mass, and productive self-sufficiency as a continental economy into a structural capability that could generate, inter alia, a dynamic growth trajectory, a reinvigoration of social citizenship, and a capacity to operate as a genuine counterweight to the

United States in international relations? In structural-functionalist terms, the abstract potentials are there. There is no reason to suppose that the Malthusian postindustrialist prediction—that Europe is now destined to suffer from Baumolitis—is correct. To the contrary, as has been argued powerfully before, Europe's industrial relations systems and systems of innovation could well provide the bases for a paradigm of post-Fordist growth that are compatible not only with the maintenance, but also with the extension, of social citizenship norms (Freyssenet, 1998; Lipietz, 1994). Some rather well known and conventional Keynesian mechanisms are missing for the institution of a mode of regulation that would enable such a trajectory of economic development (Lipietz, 1994; Boyer, 2000). To be sure, with an impending ecological crisis; radically transformed gender relations requiring new reproductive welfare services; and a vast, underdeveloped European periphery in the "wild East" and the Middle East, there is no shortage of horizons of expansion of what we call "Kaldor-Verdoorn effects" (see Chapter 3). But it is exactly in this context that the institutional design of the EMU, reflecting the deeper transatlantic structural power configuration, is so debilitating.

There is no doubt, apart from export-oriented, beggar-thy-neighbor niche strategies of the privileged few, that national responses face limitations more dire than the current European halfway house. While there is a legitimate debate to be had over the extent to which globalization is an objective force or not, we can at least agree that neoliberal power relations intolerably raise the stakes of interventionist alternative policies for any one individual European state. This leaves a continent-wide strategy as the only viable alternative, and, to be sure, some sort of monetary union would need to be part of the answer. However, we hold to be fanciful any belief of the current EMU turning into such a monetary union through some sort of benevolent spillover effect or, for that matter, dialectical dynamic whereby there is an Euclidian relationship between contradictions and their transcendence. Current arrangements that prevent monetary policy from seriously supporting any sort of fiscal policy (whether through an expansion of the European budget or coordination of the national budget) or investment policy, through a radically beefed-up European Investment Bank, are firmly entrenched in the treaties and require unanimity to be changed. Even more fundamentally, the problems generated by the current configuration are fragmenting rather than uniting the interests of member states. Short of a cataclysmic collapse of the current Euro-US economic relationship—which would be highly detrimental to the majority of Europeans in the still-prosperous core—at least for the foreseeable future, any change in this direction is highly unlikely. Hence, rather than spillover and benevolent dialectics, Europe's current relationship with the United States is better characterized with reference to a Weberian iron cage; an iron cage sufficiently gold-gilded for an adequate number not to challenge the transatlantic relation, especially given the lack of a compelling alternative. It is far more likely that Europe will continue, more or less quickly, to slide into ever more privatized, populist, atavistic, and parochial politics, internally as well as in relation to its peripheral neighbors. This will be truly a Europe at bay, where the fortuitous balance between capitalism and democracy will rest on increasingly precarious foundations.

Notes

1. See especially Majone (1996). As Moravcsik writes, "The recent 'politicization' of the EU, which many treat as an overwhelming and irresistible force, was in fact a self-inflicted wound. The perverse consequences are there for all to see. A better strategy, pragmatically and normatively, would be to *depoliticize* European constitutional evolution through an incremental, piecemeal strategy of implementing effective policies and modest institutional reforms—the 'Europe of results' of which Commission President Barroso has recently spoken. Were it not for needless constitutional debate, many of the domestic constraints on reform might not exist" (2006b: p. 237).

References

Abdelal, R. (2006) "Writing the Rules of Global Finance: France, Europe, and Capital Liberalization." *Review of International Political Economy* 13:1.

Albo, G. (1994) "'Competitive Austerity' and the Impasse of Capitalist Employment Policy." In R. Miliband and L. Panitch, eds., *Between Globalism and Nationalism: The Socialist Register 1994*. London: Merlin Press.

Allison, G. (1972) *The Essence of Decision*. Boston: Little, Brown.

Amin, A. (1994) "Post-Fordism: Models, Fantasies and Phantoms of Transition." In A. Amin, ed., *Post-Fordism: A Reader*. Oxford: Blackwell.

Anderson, P. (1997) "The Europe to Come." In P. Anderson and P. Gowan, eds., *The Question of Europe*. London: Verso.

Andrews, D. (1993) "The Global Origins of the Maastricht Treaty on EMU: Closing the Window of Opportunity." In A. Cafruny and G. Rosenthal, eds., *The State of the European Community*, vol. 2 of *The Maastricht Debates and Beyond*. Boulder, Colo.: Lynne Rienner.

Arrighi, G. (1994) *The Long Twentieth Century*. London: Verso.

Arrighi, G. (2005a) "Hegemony Unravelling: Part 1." *New Left Review* 32.

Arrighi, G. (2005b) "Hegemony Unravelling: Part 2." *New Left Review* 33.

Arts, W., and J. Gelissen. (2002) "Three Worlds of Welfare Capitalism or More? A State-of-the-Art Report." *Journal of European Social Policy* 12:2.

Asia Times. (2006) February 23.

Atkins, R. (2006) "Europe: Bank Releases Data to Back Bonds Policy." *Financial Times*. February 10.

Baghat, G. (2002) "Pipeline Diplomacy: The Geopolitics of the Caspian Sea Region." *International Studies Perspectives* 3:3.

Baker, R. (2006) "The New, Old Face of Asia." *Stratfor Geopolitical Intelligence Report*. November 16.

Barber, T. (2005) "Italian Premier Rounds on the Euro." *Financial Times*. July 29.

Baudrillard, J. (2005) "Holy Europe." *New Left Review* 33. May/June.

Baumol, W. (1967) "The Macroeconomics of Unbalanced Growth." *American Economic Review* 57.

Baun, M. (1996) "The Maastricht Treaty as High Politics: Germany, France, and European Integration." *Political Science Quarterly* 111:1.

BBC World Service. (2007) *World View of United States Role Goes from Bad to Worse,* http://www.worldpublicopinion.org/PIPA/articles. January 27.

Becker, U. (2000) "A 'Dutch Model': Employment Growth by Corporatist Consensus and Wage Restraint: A Critical Account of an Idyllic View." *New Political Economy* 6:1.

Beland, D., and R. Hansen. (2000) "Reforming the French Welfare State: Solidarity, Social Exclusion and the Three Crises of Citizenship." *West European Politics* 23:1.

Bendix, R. (1977) *Nation Building and Citizenship: Studies of Our Changing Social Order.* Berkeley: University of California Press.

Benoit B., and R. Milne. (2006) "Germany's Best-Kept Secret: How Its Exporters Are Beating the World." *Financial Times.* May 19.

Bernstein, R., and M. Gordon. (2006) "Berlin File Says Germany's Spies Aided U.S. in Iraq." *New York Times.* March 2.

Beunderman, M. (2006) "Poland Compares German-Russian Pipeline to Nazi-Soviet Pact." *EUobserver.* May 2.

Bieling, H-J. (2003) "Social Forces in the Making of the New European Economy: The Case of Financial Market Integration." *New Political Economy* 8:2.

Bieling, H-J., and T. Schulten. (2003) "'Competitive Restructuring' and Industrial Relations with the European Union: Corporatist Involvement and Beyond." In A. Cafruny and M. Ryner, eds., *A Ruined Fortress? Neoliberal Hegemony and Transformation in Europe.* Lanham, Md.: Rowman & Littlefield.

Bilmes, L., and J. Stiglitz. (2006) "The Economic Costs of the Iraq War: An Appraisal Three Years After the Beginning of the Conflict." National Bureau of Economic Research Working Paper no. W12054 (Washington, D.C.).

Block, F. (1977) *The Origins of International Economic Disorder: A Study of U.S. International Monetary Policy from World War II to the Present.* Berkeley: University of California Press.

Bohle, D. (2005) "The EU and Eastern Europe: Failing the Test as a Better World Power." In L. Panitch and C. Leys, eds., *The Empire Reloaded: Socialist Register 2005.* London: Merlin Press.

Bolkestein, F. (2001) "European Competitiveness." Ambrosetti Annual Forum, Cernobbio, http://europa.eu.int/comm/internal_market/en/speeches/pch373.htm. September 8.

Boltho, A. (2003) "What's Wrong with Europe?" *New Left Review* 22.

Bordonaro, F. (2005a) "Bulgaria, Rumania and the Changing Structure of the Black Sea Geopolitics." *Power and Interest News Report (PINR).* May 20.

Bordonaro, F. (2005b) "Intelligence Brief: U.S. Military Bases in the Black Sea Region." *Power and Interest News Report (PINR).* November 19.

Bordonaro, F. (2006a) "Kazakhstan and the 'New Great Game.'" *Asia Times.* March 10.

Bordonaro, F. (2006b) "Asia's Dawning Multipolar System Increases Australia's Geopolitical Importance." *Power and Interest News Report (PINR).* June 14.

Boudette, N. (2004) "As Jobs Head to Eastern Europe Unions in West Start to Bend." *Wall Street Journal.* March 11.

Bourdieu, P. (1977) *Outline of a Theory of Practice.* Cambridge: Cambridge University Press.

Boyer, R. (1990) "The Impact of the Single Market on Labour and Employment: A Discussion of Macro-economic Approaches in Light of Research in Labour Economics." *Labour and Society* 15:2.

Boyer, R. (1995) "Capital-Labour Relations in OECD: From the Fordist Golden Age to Contrasted Trajectories." In J. Schor and J. Il You, eds., *Capital, the State and Labour: A Global Perspective.* Aldershot, UK: Edward Elgar.

Boyer, R. (2000) "The Unanticipated Fallout of European Monetary Union: The Political and Institutional Deficits of the Euro." In C. Crouch, ed., *After the Euro.* Oxford: Oxford University Press.

Boyer, R., and P. Petit. (1991) "Technical Change, Cumulative Causation and Growth." In Organization of Economic Cooperation and Development (OECD), Technology and Productivity Programme, *Technology and Productivity: The Challenge of Economic Policy.* Paris: OECD.

Brenner, R. (2006) *The Economics of Global Turbulence.* London: Verso.

Briggs, A. (1969 [2000]) "The Welfare State in Historical Perspective." In F. Castles and C. Pierson, eds., *The Welfare State Reader.* Cambridge, UK: Polity Press.

Brzezinski, Z. (1997a) "A Geostrategy for Eurasia." *Foreign Affairs* 76:5.

Brzezinski, Z. (1997b) *The Grand Chessboard: American Primacy and Its Geostrategic Imperatives.* New York: Basic Books.

Brzezinski, Z. (2004) *The Choice: Global Domination or Global Leadership.* New York: Basic Books.

Buchele, R., and J. Christiansen. (1998) "Do Employment and Income Security Cause Unemployment?" *Cambridge Journal of Economics* 22:1.

Buti, M., D. Franco, and H. Onenga. (1998) "Fiscal Discipline and Flexibility in EMU: The Implementation of the Stability and Growth Pact." *Oxford Review of Economic Policy* 14:3.

Cafruny, A. (1990) "A Gramscian Concept of Declining Hegemony: Stages of U.S. Power and the Evolution of International Economic Relations." In D. Rapkin, ed., *World Leadership and Hegemony.* Boulder, Colo.: Lynne Rienner.

Cafruny, A. (2002) "Transatlantic Trade and Monetary Relations: The Nature and Limits of Conflict." *International Spectator* 37:3.

Cafruny, A. (2003) "The Geopolitics of U.S. Hegemony in Europe: From the Break-Up of Yugoslavia to the War in Iraq." In A. Cafruny and M. Ryner, eds., *A Ruined Fortress? Neoliberal Hegemony and Transformation in Europe.* Lanham, Md.: Rowman & Littlefield.

Cafruny, A., and M. Ryner. (2003) *A Ruined Fortress? Neoliberal Hegemony and Transformation in Europe.* Lanham, Md.: Rowman & Littlefield.

Caldwell, C. (2005) "The Final Round for Party Politics." *Financial Times.* November 19.

Callaway, D. (2006) "Wall Street Plays the Scare Card: Global Leadership of U.S. Banks Not Threatened." *Marketwatch.* December 7.

Calleo, D. (2003) "Balancing America: Europe's International Duties." *International Politics and Society* 1.

Calleo, D., ed. (1982) *The Imperious Economy.* Cambridge, Mass.: Harvard University Press.

Calmfors, L., and J. Driffil. (1988) "Bargaining Structure, Corporatism and Macroeconomic Performance." *Economic Policy* 6.

Cameron, A., and R. Palan. (1999) "The Imagined Economy: Mapping Transformations in the Contemporary State." *Millennium: Journal of International Studies* 28:2.

Cameron, D. R. (1997) "Economic and Monetary Union: Underlying Imperatives and Third-Stage Dilemmas." *Journal of European Public Policy* 4:3.

Campanella, M. (2002) "Euro Weakness and ECB Governance: A Strategic Institutionalist Perspective." In M. Campanella and S. Eiffinger, eds., *EU Economic Governance and Globalization.* London: Edward Elgar.

Caporaso, J. (1996) "The EU and Forms of State: Westphalian, Regulatory, or Postmodern?" *Journal of Common Market Studies* 34:1.

Caporaso, J., ed. (2000) *Continuity and Change in the Westphalian Order.* New York: Routledge.

Cassen, B. (2005) "Europe: No Is Not a Disaster." *Le Monde Diplomatique* (English-lang. edition).

Center for European Policy Reform (CEPR). (2002) "Surviving the Slowdown." *Monitoring the European Central Bank* 4.

Center for Strategic and International Studies (CSIS). (2005) *European Defense Integration: Bridging the Gap Between Strategy and Capabilities.* Washington, D.C.: CSIS.

Charchedi, G. (2001) *For Another Europe: A Class Analysis of European Economic Integration.* London: Verso.

Clark, G. L. (2001) "Requiem for a National Ideal? Social Solidarity, the Crisis of French Social Security, and the Role of Global Financial Markets." *Environment and Planning A* 33:1.

Clasen, J. (1994) "Social Security: The Core of the German Employment Centred Social State." In J. Clasen and R. Freeman, eds., *Social Policy in Germany.* London: Harvester Wheatsheaf.

Clayton, R., and J. Pontusson. (1998) "Welfare State Retrenchment Revisited." *World Politics* 51:1.

Clift, B. (2003) "The Changing Political Economy of France: *Dirigisme* Under Duress." In A. Cafruny and M. Ryner, eds., *A Ruined Fortress? Neoliberal Hegemony and Transformation in Europe.* Lanham, Md.: Rowman & Littlefield.

Codita, C. (2005) "Romania, U.S. Sign Military Base Agreement." *Deutsche Welle.* December 7.

Cohen, B. (2003) "Global Currency Rivalry: Can the Euro Ever Rival the Dollar?" Paper 8, Global and International Studies Program, University of California at Santa Barbara.

Connolly, W. E. (1993) *The Terms of Political Discourse.* Princeton, N.J.: Princeton University Press.

Constitutional Treaty for Europe (TCE). (2004) Brussels.

Council of the European Union (CEU). (2005) *Improving the Implementation of the Stability and Growth Pact.* 7423/05 UEM 97 ECOFIN 104.

Cox, R. W. (1987) *Production, Power, and World Order: Social Forces in the Making of History.* New York: Columbia University Press.

Cox, R. W. (1992) "Towards a Post-Hegemonic Conceptualization of World Order: Reflections on the Relevancy of Ibn Khaldun." In E-O. Czempiel and J. Rosenau, eds., *Governance Without Government: Order and Change in World Politics.* Cambridge: Cambridge University Press.

Crouch, C. (2000) "Introduction: The Political and Institutional Deficits of European Monetary Union." In C. Crouch, ed., *After the Euro.* Oxford: Oxford University Press.

Cutler, C. (2003) *Private Power and Global Authority.* Cambridge: Cambridge University Press.

Davies, P. (2002) *The Extreme Right in France, 1789 to the Present: From de Maistre to Le Pen.* Basingstoke, UK: Palgrave Macmillan.

De Grauwe, P. (2003) *The Economics of Monetary Union.* 5th ed. Oxford: Oxford University Press.

De Grauwe, P. (2006a) "Economists Call for Political Union to Prevent Euro Collapse." *EUobserver.* April 24.

De Grauwe, P. (2006b) "Germany's Pay Policy Points to a Eurozone Design Flaw." *Financial Times.* May 5.

De Grauwe, P. (2006c) "What Have We Learnt About Monetary Integration Since the Maastricht Treaty?" *Journal of Common Market Studies* 44:4.

De Haas, M. (2006) "Current Geostrategy in the South Caucasus." *Power and Interest News Report (PINR).* December 15.

Democratic Leadership Council. (2006) *A Winning Strategy: This Time, Democrats Can Win the National Security Debate with Positive Ideas for Protecting America,* http://www.dlc.org.

Deppe, F. (2004) "Habermas' Manifesto for a European Renaissance: A Critique." In L. Panitch and C. Leys, eds., *The Empire Reloaded: Socialist Register 2005.* London: Merlin Press.

Derrida, J., and J. Habermas. (2003) "Nach dem Krieg: Die Wiedergeburt Europas." *Frankfurter Allgemeine Zeitung.* May 31.

Deubner, C., U. Rehfeld, and F. Schlupp (1992) "Franco-German Relations Within the International Division of Labour: Interdependence, Divergence or Structural Dominance?" In W. Graf, ed., *The Internationalization of the German Political Economy: Evolution of a Hegemonic Project.* New York: St. Martin's Press.

Deutsche Welle. (2005) "Romania, U.S. Sign Military Base Agreement." December 7.

Dicken, P. (1998) *Global Shift: Transforming the World Economy,* 3d ed. London: Paul Chapman.

Duménil, G., and D. Lévy. (2001) "Costs and Benefits of Neoliberalism: A Class Analysis." *Review of International Political Economy* 8:4.

Duménil, G., and D. Lévy. (2003) "Neo-Liberal Dynamics: Imperial Dynamics." Paper presented at the Conference on Global Regulation, University of Sussex. May 29–31.

Duménil, G., and D. Lévy. (2004) "The Economics of US Imperialism at the Turn of the 21st Century." *Review of International Political Economy* 11:4.

Dunford, M. (2005) "Old Europe, New Europe, and the USA: Comparative Economic Performance, Inequality, and Market-Led Models of Development." *European Urban and Regional Studies* 12:2.

Dyson, K. (2000) *The Politics of the Euro-Zone: Stability or Breakdown?* Oxford: Oxford University Press.

Dyson, K., and K. Featherstone. (1999) *The Road to Maastricht: Negotiating Economic and Monetary Union.* Oxford: Oxford University Press.

Economist. (2004) "Je t'aime, ich auch nicht," June 6.

Economist. (2006a) "European Energy Markets." Special report. February 11.

Economist. (2006b) "Changing Places: Britain's National Defence Champion May Soon Be American." October 26.

Economist Intelligence Unit (ECI). (2006) *World Investment Prospects 2006.* London: ECI.

Eichengreen, B. (1992) "Is Europe an Optimal Currency Area?" In S. Borner and H. Grubel, eds., *The European Community After 1992.* London: Macmillan.

Emerson, M., M. Aujean, M. Catinat, P. Goybet, and A. Jaquemin. (1988) *The Economics of 1992: The EC Commission's Assessment of the Economic Effects of Completing the Internal Market.* Oxford: Oxford University Press.

Esping-Andersen, G. (1990) *The Three Worlds of Welfare Capitalism.* Cambridge, UK: Polity Press.

Esping-Andersen, G. (1996) "Welfare States Without Work: The Impasse of Labour Shedding and Familialism in Continental European Social Policy." In G. Esping-Andersen, ed., *Welfare States in Transition: National Adaptations in Global Economies.* London: Sage/UNRISD.

Esping-Andersen, G. (1999) *The Social Foundations of Postindustrial Economies.* Oxford: Oxford University Press.

EUobserver. (2005) "U.S. Defense Industry Concerned by Possible French No." May 27, www.euobserver.com.

EUobserver. (2006a) "EU Energy Policy Encounters Difficulties." February 8, www.euobserver.com.

EUobserver. (2006b) "Brussels Upbeat About Economic Reform Drive." December 12, www.euobserver.com.

European Commission (EC). (1990) *One Market, One Money.* Luxembourg: Office for the Official Publications of the EC.

European Commission (EC). (1993) *Growth, Competitiveness and Employment: The Challenges and the Ways Forward into the 21st Century.* White paper. Com (93) 700. December.

European Commission (EC). (1996) *The 1996 Single Market Review: Background Information for the Report to the Council and the European Parliament.* Brussels: European Commission.

European Commission (EC). (2001) "The Right Regulatory Environment: Action Points for Stockholm." Brussels. March 23–24.

European Commission (EC). (2003a) *European Defence; Industrial and Market Issues: Towards an EU Defence Equipment Policy.* 3.11.2004 Com (2003) 133 final.

European Commission (EC). (2003b) *European Economy* 6. Luxembourg: Office for the Official Publications of the EC.

European Commission (EC). (2003c) *Second Progress Report on Economic and Social Cohesion.* Brussels: European Commission.

European Commission (EC). (2005a) *Eurobarometer 64: Public Opinion in the European Union; National Report: Germany.* Brussels: European Commission.

European Commission (EC). (2005b) "Proposal for a Council Regulation: Amending Regulation (EC) No. 1466/97 on the Strengthening of the Surveillance of Budgetary Positions and the Surveillance and Coordination of Economic Policies." 20.4.2005 Com (2005) 154 final.

European Commission (EC). (2005c) "Proposal for a Council Regulation: Amending Regulation (EC) No. 1466/97 on Speeding Up and Clarifying the Implementation of the Excessive Deficit Procedure." 20.4.2005 Com (2005) 155 final.

European Commission (EC). (2006a) *The European Economy.* Spring, Brussels: European Commission.

European Commission (EC). (2006b) "European Energy Policy Green Paper."

European Commission (EC). (2006c) *Quarterly Report on the Euro Area* 5:3.

European Council. (2000) *Presidency Conclusions, Lisbon European Council 23rd and 24th March.* Brussels: European Council.

European Parliament (EP). (2006) *Interim Report on the Alleged Use of European Countries by the CIA for the Transportation and Illegal Detention of Prisoners.* Rapporteur, G. Fava. A6-0213/2006. May 15.

Eurostat, European Commission. (2001) *Structural Indicators: Labour Productivity.* December 11, http://epp.eurostat.ec.europa.eu.

Farrell, D. (2005) "The U.S. Trade Deficit Does Not Spell Doom." *Financial Times.* February 10.

Feldstein, M. (1997) "EMU and International Conflict." *Foreign Affairs* 76.

Feldstein, M. (2006) "Why Uncle Sam's Bonanza Might Not Be All That It Seems." *Financial Times.* January 10.

Ferrera, M. (1996) "The 'Southern' Model of Welfare in Social Europe?" *Journal of European Social Policy* 6:1, pp. 17–37.

Financial Times. (1991) July 1, p. 2.

Financial Times. (2005a) "Messy Gridlock." Editorial comment. March 10.

Financial Times. (2005b) "Death of a Pact." March 22.

Financial Times. (2005c) "Go-Ahead for 900km Euro Pipeline to Ease Pressure on Bosphorus." April 12.

Financial Times. (2005d) "Poland Ready to March on to World Stage." December 30.

Financial Times. (2006a) "VW to Cut 20,000 Jobs over Next Three Years." February 11/12.

Financial Times. (2006b) "China." Special report. December 12.

Financial Times. (2007) "Interview: Dominique de Villepin." February 6.

Fondazione Rodolfo Debendetti (FRD). (2005) Social Reforms Database. http://www.frdb.org/documentazione/centro_doc.php. Accessed April 4.

Freyberg-Inan, A. (2005) "World System Theory: A Bird's-Eye View of the World Capitalist Order." In Jennifer Sterling-Folker, ed., *Making Sense of International Relations Theory.* Boulder, Colo.: Lynne Rienner.

Freyssenet, M. (1998) "'Reflective Production': An Alternative to Mass Production and Lean Production?" *Economic and Industrial Democracy* 19:1.

Frieden, J. (1991) "Invested Interests: The Politics of National Economic Policies in a World of Global Finance." *International Organization* 45:4.

Frieden, J., D. Gros, and E. Jones. (1998) *The New Political Economy of the EMU.* Lanham, Md.: Rowman & Littlefield.

Ganssmann, H. (2004) "Germany: Capital Flees." *Le Monde Diplomatique* (English-lang. edition). February.

Gerschenkron, A. (1962) *Economic Backwardness in Historical Perspective.* Cambridge, Mass.: Harvard University Press.

Giavazzi F., and M. Pagano. (1988) "The Advantage of Tying One's Hands: EMS Discipline and Central Bank Credibility." *European Economic Review* 32:5.

Giavazzi, F., and M. Pagano. (1990) "Can Severe Fiscal Contractions Be Expansionary? Tales of Two Small European Countries." In O. Blanchard and S. Fischer, eds., *NBER Macroeconomics Annual.* Cambridge, Mass.: MIT Press.

Gill, S. (1990) *American Hegemony and the Trilateral Commission.* Cambridge: Cambridge University Press.

Gill, S. (1998) "European Governance and New Constitutionalism: Economic and Monetary Union and Alternatives to Disciplinary Neo-Liberalism in Europe." *New Political Economy* 3:1.

Gill, S., and D. Law. (1989) "Global Hegemony and the Structural Power of Capital." *International Studies Quarterly* 33:4.

Gilpin, R. (1973) *U.S. Power and the Multinational Corporations.* New York: Basic Books.

GlobalSecurity.org. (2006) http://www.globalsecurity.org.

GlobeScan. Program on International Policy Attitudes (PIPA). (2005) http://www.pipa.org/onlineReports/Europe/040605/html/new.

Glyn, A. (2001) "Inequalities of Employment and Wages in the OECD Countries." *Oxford Bulletin of Economics and Statistics* 63:1.

Glyn, A., A. Lipietz, A. Hughes, and A. Singh. (1990) "The Rise and the Fall of the Golden Age." In S. Marglin and J. Schor, eds., *The Golden Age of Capitalism.* Oxford: Clarendon.

Goldgeier, J. (1999) *Not Whether But When: The U.S. Decision to Enlarge NATO.* Washington, D.C.: The Brookings Institution.

Golub, P. (2004) "Imperial Politics, Imperial Will, and the Crisis of U.S. Hegemony." *Review of International Political Economy* 11:4.

Gordon, R. (2004) *Why Was Europe Left at the Station When America's Productivity Locomotive Departed?* NBER working paper 10661. Washington, D.C. August.

Gough, I. (1996) "Social Welfare and Competitiveness." *New Political Economy* 1:2.

Goul Andersen, J. (2003) "Citizenship Politics: Activation, Welfare and Employment in Denmark." Paper presented at the conference "Social Governance in the Global Era: Beyond 20th Century Social Democracy." Hokkaido University, Sapporo, Japan. October 14–17.

Goul Andersen, J. (2007) "The Danish Welfare State as 'Politics for Markets': Combining Equality and Competitiveness in a Global Economy." *New Political Economy* 12:1.

Gowan, P. (1996) "Eastern Europe, Western Power, and Neoliberalism." *New Left Review* 216 (old series edition).

Gowan, P. (1999) *The Global Gamble: Washington's Faustian Bid for World Dominance.* London: Verso.

Gowan, P. (2006) "A Radical Realist." *New Left Review* 41. September–October.

Grahl, J. (2001) "Globalized Finance: The Challenge to the Euro." *New Left Review* 8.

Grahl, J. (2005a) "The European Union and American Power." In L. Panitch and C. Leys, eds., *The Empire Reloaded: Socialist Register 2005.* London: Merlin Press.

Grahl, J. (2005b) "Europe's Inflexible Bank." *Le Monde Diplomatique* (English-lang. edition). July.

Gramsci, A. (1971) *Selections from the Prison Notebooks.* Q. Hoare and G. Nowell Smith, eds. and trans. New York: International.

Greffrath, M. (2005) "Germany: New Left, Old Right." *Le Monde Diplomatique* (English-lang. edition). September.

Gresh, A. (2006) "Middle East: France Rejoins the Pack." *Le Monde Diplomatique* (English-lang. edition). June.

Gros, D., T. Mayer, and A. Ubide. (2005) *Euro at Risk.* Brussels: Centre for European Policy Studies.

Gross, D. (2007) "Does It Even Matter if the U.S. Has a Cold?" *New York Times,* May 6.

Guha, R. (1992) "Dominance Without Hegemony and Its Historiography." In R. Guha, ed., *Subaltern Studies VI.* New Delhi.

Guardian. (2002) December 27.

Habermas, J. (1975) *Legitimation Crisis.* Boston: Beacon Press.

Hale, D. (2005) "Could Italy Be First to Leave the Euro?" *European Affairs.*

Hall, P., and R. Franzese. (1998) "Mixed Signals: Central Bank Independence, Coordinated Wage Bargaining and European Monetary Union." *International Organization* 52:3.

Harvey, D. (1990) *The Condition of Postmodernity.* Oxford: Blackwell.

Harvey, D. (2003) *The New Imperialism.* Oxford: Oxford University Press.

Haseler, S. (2004) *Superstate: The New Europe and Its Challenge to America.* London: I. B. Taurus.

Häusler, J., and J. Hirsch (1989) "Political Regulation: The Crisis of Fordism and the Transformation of the Party System in West Germany." In M. Gottdiener and N. Komninos, eds., *Capitalist Development and Crisis Theory.* New York: St. Martin's Press.

Helleiner, E. (1994) *States and the Re-emergence of Global Finance.* Ithaca, N.Y.: Cornell University Press.

Hemerijck, A. (2002) "The Self-Transformation of the European Social Model(s)." *International Politics and Society* 4.

Hirst, P., and G. Thompson. (1996) *Globalization in Question.* Cambridge, UK: Polity Press.

Hix, S. (1999) *The Political System of the European Union.* London: Macmillan.

Holland, S. (1979) *Uncommon Market: Capital, Class and Power in the European Community.* London: Macmillan.

Hollingsworth, R., and R. Boyer, eds. (1997) *Contemporary Capitalism: The Embeddedness of Institutions.* Cambridge: Cambridge University Press.

Holman, O. (2001) "The Enlargement of the EU Towards Central and Eastern Europe: The Role of Supranational and Transnational Actors." In A. Bieler and A. D. Morton, eds., *Social Forces in the Making of the New Europe: The Restructuring of European Social Relations in the Global Political Economy.* Basingstoke, UK: Palgrave Macmillan.

Holman, O. (2004a) "Asymmetrical Regulation and Multidimensional Governance in the European Union." *Review of International Political Economy* 11:4.

Holman, O. (2004b) "Integrating Peripheral Europe: The Different Roads to 'Security and Stability' in Southern and Central Europe." *Journal of International Relations and Development* 7:2.

Holman, O., and K. van der Pijl. (2003) "Structure and Process in Transnational European Business." In A. Cafruny and M. Ryner, eds., *A Ruined Fortress? Neoliberal Hegemony and Transformation in Europe.* Lanham, Md.: Rowman & Littlefield.

Holtz-Eakin, D. (2006) "How to Determine Whether the War Is Worth It." *Financial Times.* February 14.

Hooghe, L., and G. Marks. (2001) *Multilevel Governance and European Integration.* Lanham, Md.: Rowman & Littlefield.

Howarth, D. (2002) "The French State in the Euro-Zone: 'Modernization' and Legitimizing *Dirigisme.*" In K. Dyson, ed., *European States and the Euro.* Oxford: Oxford University Press.

Hufbauer, G., and F. Neumann. (2002) *US-EU Trade and Investment: An American Perspective.* Washington, D.C.: Institute for International Economics.

Hufbauer, I. (2006) "Making the Social Productive and Neoliberalism Popular: The Concept of the European Social Model in the Discourse of EU Institutions." Paper presented to European Sociological Association workshop "Beyond the Crisis of the European Project?" Free University of Amsterdam. September.

Hutton, W. (2002) *The World We're In.* New York: Little, Brown.

Inan-Freybourg, A. (2005) "World System Theory: A Bird's-Eye View of the World Capitalist Order." In J. Sterling-Folker, ed., *Making Sense of International Relations Theory.* Boulder, Colo.: Lynne Rienner.

International Monetary Fund (IMF). (2004) "Euro Area Policies: Selected Issues." *IMF Country Report,* No. 04/234.

Interpress Service (IPS). (2005) "Powell Aide Blasts Rice, Cheney-Rumsfeld 'Cabal.'" October 20.

Interpress Service (IPS). (2006) "In Public's Eyes Iran Biggest Foreign Menace." February 10.

Issing, O. (2002) "On Macroeconomic Policy Co-ordination in EMU." *Journal of Common Market Studies* 40:2.

Iversen, T., and A. Wren. (1998) "Equality, Employment and Budgetary Restraint: The Trilemma of the Service Economy." *World Politics* 50:4.

Jackson, B. (2006) "The 'Soft War' for Europe's East." *Policy Review* 137.

Jervis, P., ed. (2005) *Resolving the European Crisis: Perspectives on the Future of the European Union.* London: Middlesex University Press.

Jessop, B. (1990) *State Theory: Putting Capitalist States in Their Place.* Cambridge, UK: Polity Press.

Jones, S. and F. Larrabee. (2005/2006). "Arming Europe." *The National Interest* 82. Winter.

Kagan, R. (2003) *Of Paradise and Power: America and Europe in the New World Order.* New York: Vintage.

Katzenstein, P. (1985) *Small States in World Markets.* Ithaca, N.Y.: Cornell University Press.

Kelly, K. (1998) *New Rules for the New Economy.* London: Fourth Estate.

Keohane, R. (1980) "The Theory of Hegemonic Stability and Changes in International Economic Regimes, 1967–77." In O. R. Holsti, et al., eds., *Changes in the International System.* Boulder, Colo.: Westview Press.

Kindleberger, C. (1973) *The World in Depression.* Berkeley: University of California Press.

Kirchgaessner, S., and B. White. (2006) "Goldman Sachs Top Alumni Wield Clout in White House." *Financial Times*. December 4.

Klare, M. (2006) "The New Geopolitics." *Monthly Review* 57:9.

Korpi, W. (2003) "Welfare-State Regress in Western Europe: Politics, Institutions, Globalization and Europeanization." *Annual Review of Sociology* 29.

Korpi, W., and J. Palme. (2003) "New Politics and Class Politics in the Context of Austerity and Globalization: Welfare-State Regress in 18 Countries 1975–1995." *American Political Science Review* 97:3.

Krugman, P. (1991) *Geography and Trade*. Cambridge, Mass.: MIT Press.

Kubosova, L. (2006) "Economists Call for Political Union to Prevent Euro's Collapse." *EUobserver.* April 24.

Kuhn, T. (1962) *The Structure of Scientific Revolutions*. Chicago: University of Chicago Press.

Kupchan, C. (2002) *The End of the American Era: U.S. Foreign Policy and the Geopolitics of the Twenty-First Century*. New York: Vintage.

Lacher, H. (2002) "Making Sense of the International System: The Promises and Pitfalls of Contemporary Marxist Theories of International Relations." In M. Rupert and H. Smith, eds., *Historical Materialism and Globalization*. London: Routledge.

Lafontaine, O. (2000) *The Heart Beats on the Left*. Cambridge, UK: Polity Press.

Lankowski, C. (1982) "Modell Deutschland and the International Regionalization of the West German State." In A. Markovits, ed., *The Political Economy of West Germany: Modell Deutschland*. New York: Praeger.

Layne, C. (2006) *The Peace of Illusions: American Grand Strategy from 1940 to the Present*. Ithaca, N.Y.: Cornell University Press.

Leborgne, D., and A. Lipietz. (1988) "New Technologies, New Modes of Regulation: Some Spatial Implications." *Environment and Planning D: Society and Space* 6:3.

Len, C. (2006) "The Growing Importance of Japan's Engagement in Asia." *Power and Interest News Report (PINR)*. February 17.

Lenin, V. (1916) *Imperialism: The Highest Stage of Capitalism*. New York: International.

Leonard, M. (2005) *Why Europe Will Run the Twenty-First Century*. London: Fourth Estate.

Levey, D., and S. Brown. (2005) "The Overstretch Myth: Can the Indispensable Nation Be a Debtor Nation?" *Foreign Affairs* 84:2.

Levy, J. (2001) "Partisan Politics and Welfare Adjustment: The Case of France." *Journal of European Public Policy* 8:2.

Lieven, A. (2004) *America Right or Wrong: An Anatomy of American Nationalism*. Oxford: Oxford University Press.

Lindberg, L., R. Alford, C. Crouch, and C. Offe, eds. (1975) *Stress and Contradiction in Modern Capitalism*. Lexington, Mass.: Lexington Books.

Lindblom, C. (1980) *Politics and Markets*. New York: Basic Books.

Lipietz, A. (1985) *Mirages and Miracles: The Crisis of Global Fordism*. London: Verso.

Lipietz, A. (1989) "The Debt Problem, European Integration and the New Phase of World Crisis." *New Left Review* 178 (old series).

Lipietz, A. (1994) *Towards a New Economic Order*. Cambridge, UK: Polity Press.

Lipietz, A. (1997) "The Post-Fordist World: Labour Relations, International Hierarchy and Global Ecology." *Review of International Political Economy* 4:1.

Lipset, S. M., and S. Rokkan. (1967 [1990]) "Cleavage Structures, Party Systems and Voter Alignments." In P. Mair, ed., *The West European Party Politics*. Oxford: Oxford University Press.

Lorentowicz, A., D. Marin, and A. Raubold. (2002) *Ownership, Capital or Outsourcing: What Drives German Investment to Eastern Europe?* Munich: Center for Economic Policy Research.

Loriaux, M. (1991) *France and Hegemony: International Change and Financial Reform*. Ithaca, N.Y.: Cornell University Press.

Lösche, P., and F. Walter (1992) *Die SPD: Klassenpartei, Volkspartei, Quotenpartei*. Darmstadt: Wissenschaftlige Buchgesellschaft.

Lukes, S. (1974) *Power: A Radical View*. London: Macmillan.

Lütz, S. (2002) *Der Staat und die Globalisierung der Finanzmarkten*. Frankfurt: Campus Verlag.

Mabbett, D., and W. Schelkle. (2005) "Bringing Macroeconomics Back into the Political Economy of Reform: The Lisbon Agenda and the 'Fiscal Philosophy' of EMU." Working paper, Center for European Policy Studies (CEPS).

MacDougall Report, Vol. I. (1977) *The Role of Public Finance in European Integration*. Brussels: European Commission.

MacKay, R. (1995) "European Integration and Public Finance: The Political Economy of Regional Support." In S. Hardy, M. Hart, L. Albrechts, and A. Katos, eds., *An Enlarged Europe*. London: Jessica Kingsley.

Magnusson, L., and B. Strath. (2001) *From the Werner Plan to the EMU; In Search of European Political Economy: Historical Perspectives and Future Prospects*. Brussels: Peter Lang.

Mahon, R. (1987) "From Fordism to ?: New Technology, Labour Markets and Unions." *Economic and Industrial Democracy* 8:1.

Mahon, R. (2007) "Swedish Model Dying of Baumols? Current Debates." *New Political Economy* 12:1.

Mair, P. (2006) "Ruling the Void: The Hollowing of Western Democracy." *New Left Review* 42.

Majone, G. (1996) "Temporal Consistency and Policy Credibility." Working paper 96/57, European University Institute, Florence.

Manow, P. (1997) "Social Insurance and German Political Economy." Discussion paper 97/2, Max Planck Institut für Gesellschaftsforschung, Leipzig.

March, J. G., and J. P. Olsen. (1989) *Rediscovering Institutions: The Organizational Basis of Politics*. New York: Free Press.

Marshall, T. H. (1950) *Citizenship and Social Class and Other Essays*. Cambridge: Cambridge University Press.

McCormack, G. (2005) "Koizumi's Coup." *New Left Review* 35.

McCormick, J. (2007) *The European Superpower*. New York: Palgrave Macmillan.

McNamara, K. (1998) *The Currency of Ideas: Monetary Politics in the EU*. Ithaca, N.Y.: Cornell University Press.

Mearsheimer, J. (2001) *The Tragedy of Great Power Politics*. New York: W. W. Norton.

Milward, A. (1992) *The European Rescue of the Nation-State.* Berkeley: University of California Press.

Milward, A., et al. (1993) *The Frontier of National Sovereignty: History and Theory 1945–1992.* London: Routledge.

Milward, A. (1994) "The Social Bases of Monetary Union?" In P. Gowan and P. Anderson, eds., *The Question of Europe.* London: Verso.

Ministry of Foreign Affairs of Japan. (2005) *U.S.-Japan Alliance: Transformation and Realignment for the Future.* Security Consultative Committee Document. Tokyo. October.

Moisi, D. (2005) "Europe Must Not Go the Way of Decadent Venice." *Financial Times.* June 12.

Moravcsik, A. (1998) *The Choice for Europe: Social Purpose and State Power from Messina to Maastricht.* Ithaca, N.Y.: Cornell University Press.

Moravcsik, A. (2006a) "Chastened Leaders Need Concrete Policy Successes." *Financial Times.* January 22.

Moravcsik, A. (2006b) "What Can We Learn from the Collapse of the European Constitutional Project?" *Politische Vierteljahresschrift* 47:2.

Moreno, L. (2000) "The Spanish Development of Southern European Welfare." In S. Kuhnle, ed., *The Survival of the Welfare State.* London: Routledge.

Munchau, W. (2004) "Europe Needs Retail Therapy." *Financial Times.* May 9.

Munchau, W. (2005) "Is the Euro Forever? As the Strains Turn to Pain, Its Foundations Look Far from Secure." *Financial Times.* June 8.

Munchau, W. (2007) "Germany Must Import Some Fresh Thinking." *Financial Times.* March 5.

Murphy, C., and R. Tooze, eds. (1991) *The New International Political Economy.* Boulder, Colo.: Lynne Rienner.

National Intelligence Council (USA) (NIC). (2004) *Mapping the Global Future: Report of the NIC's 2020 Project.* Washington, D.C.: National Intelligence Council.

National Security Advisory Group (NSAG). (2006) *The U.S. Military: Under Strain and at Risk.* Washington, D.C.

New York Times. (2007) January 12.

Nickel, S. (1997) "Unemployment and Labour Market Rigidities: Europe vs. North America." *Journal of Economic Perspectives* 11:3.

Norris, R., and H. Kristensen. (2006) "Where the Bombs Are, 2006." *Bulletin of the Atomic Scientists* 62:6.

Nye, J. (2002) "A Whole New Ballgame." *Financial Times.* December 28.

Nye, J. (2003) "Europe Is Too Powerful to Be Ignored." *Financial Times.* March 10.

Nye, J. (2004) *Soft Power: The Means to Success in World Politics.* Cambridge, Mass.: Public Affairs.

Oakley, D., and G. Tett. (2007) "Euro Displaces Dollar in Bond Markets." *Financial Times.* January 14.

Obama '08. (2007) Remarks of Senator Obama to the Chicago Council on Foreign Affairs, http://www.mybarackobama.com, April 23.

Offe, C. (1985) *Contradictions of the Welfare State.* Cambridge, Mass.: MIT Press.

Offe, C. (1997) "Democracy Against the Welfare State?" In *Modernity and the State,* pp. 147–182. Cambridge, UK: Polity Press.

Ohmae, K. (1990) *The Borderless World.* New York: Collins.

Organisation for Economic Co-operation and Development (OECD). (1988) *New Technology in the 1990s: A Socio-Economic Strategy.* Paris: OECD.

Organisation for Economic Co-operation and Development (OECD). (1999) *Historical Statistics.* Paris: OECD.

Organisation for Economic Co-operation and Development (OECD). (2000) *Employment Outlook.* Paris: OECD.

Organisation for Economic Co-operation and Development (OECD). (2002) *Economic Surveys 2001–2002: Euro Area.* Paris: OECD.

Organisation for Economic Co-operation and Development (OECD). (2003) *Economic Surveys 2002–2003: Euro Area.* Paris: OECD.

Organisation for Economic Co-operation and Development (OECD). (2004) *Economic Outlook 75.* Paris: OECD.

Organisation for Economic Co-operation and Development (OECD). (2005) *Economic Outlook 78.* Paris: OECD.

Organisation for Economic Co-operation and Development (OECD). (2006) *Economic Outlook 80.* Paris: OECD.

Organisation for Economic Co-operation and Development (OECD). (2007) *Economic Survey of the Euro Area 2007.* Paris: OECD.

Organski, A., and J. Kugler. (1981) *The War Ledger.* Chicago: University of Chicago Press.

Padoa-Schioppa, T. (1997) "Engineering the Single Currency." In P. Gowan and P. Anderson, eds., *The Question of Europe.* London: Verso.

Palier, B. (2000) "'Defrosting' the French Welfare State." *West European Politics* 23:2.

Panitch, L. (1994) "Globalisation and the State." In R. Miliband and L. Panitch, eds., *Between Globalism and Nationalism: The Socialist Register 1994.* London: Merlin Press.

Panitch, L., and S. Gindin. (2005) "Superintending Global Capital." *New Left Review* 35.

Pant, H. (2006) "U.S.-India Nuclear Deal: The End Game Begins." *Power and Interest News Report (PINR).* January 27.

Parboni, R. (1982) *The Dollar and Its Rivals: Recession, Inflation and International Finance.* London: Verso.

Parker, G. (2005) "EU Attempts to Reform Stability Pact Break Down." *Financial Times.* March 9.

Parker, G. (2006) "Berlin Accuses Vienna of 'Fiscal Dumping.'" *Financial Times.* April 8.

Parker, G., and R. Atkins. (2006) "Eurozone 'Reaping Benefits of Reform.'" *Financial Times.* September 29.

Parker, G., and H. Simonian. (2006) "Austria to Pose Questions of Europe's Identity." *Financial Times.* January 26.

Patten, C. (2006) *Cousins and Strangers: America, Britain, and Europe in a New Century.* London: Times Books.

Petrakos, G., G. Maier, and G. Gorzelak, eds. (2000) *Integration and Transition in Europe: The Economic Geography of Interaction.* London: Routledge.

Pierson, P. (1996) "The Path to European Integration: A Historical Institutionalist Analysis." *Comparative Political Studies* 29:2.

Pierson, P. (2001) "Post-industrial Pressures on Mature Welfare States." In P. Pierson, ed., *The New Politics of the Welfare State*. Oxford: Oxford University Press.

Polackova, L. (2004) Multilevel Governance in European Economic Space: The Case of Capital Adequacy Regulation. Ph.D. thesis, School of International Studies, Brunel University, London.

Posen, A. (2005a) "Can Rubinomics Work in the Eurozone?" In A. Posen, ed., *The Euro at Five: Ready for a Global Role?* Special report 18. Washington, D.C.: Institute for International Economics.

Posen, A. (2005b) "Overview: The Euro's Success Within Limits." In A. Posen, ed., *The Euro at Five: Ready for a Global Role?* Special report 18. Washington, D.C.: Institute for International Economics.

Poulantzas, N. (1973) *Political Power and Social Classes.* London: New Left Books.

Poulantzas, N. (1974) "Internationalisation of Capitalist Relations and the Nation State." *Economy and Society* 2:1.

Poulantzas, N. (1978) *State, Power, Socialism.* London: New Left Books.

Quinlan, J. P. (2003) *Drifting Apart or Growing Together? The Primacy of the Transatlantic Economy.* Baltimore, Md.: Paul H. Nitze School of Advanced International Relations, Johns Hopkins University.

Ramet, S. (1996) *Balkan Babel: The Disintegration of Yugoslavia from the Death of Tito to Ethnic War.* Boulder, Colo.: Westview.

Reid, T. (2005) *The United States of Europe: The Superpower No-One Talks About.* New York: Penguin.

Reid, T. R. (2004) *The United States of Europe: The New Superpower and the End of American Supremacy.* New York: Penguin.

Rhodes, M. (2002) "Why EMU Is—or May Be—Good for European Welfare States." In K. Dyson, ed., *European States and the Euro.* Oxford: Oxford University Press.

Riemer, J. (1982) "Alterations in the Design of Model Germany: Critical Innovations in the Policy Machinery for Economic Steering." In A. Markovits, ed., *The Political Economy of West Germany: Modell Deutschland.* New York: Praeger.

Rifkin, J. (2004) *European Dream: How Europe's Vision of the Future is Quietly Eclipsing the American Dream.* Cambridge, UK: Polity Press.

Roach, S. (2007) "Hope for Global Decoupling Lies with the US Consumer." *Financial Times.* May 8.

Robinson, W., and J. Harris. (2000) "Toward a Global Ruling Class: Globalization and the Transnational Capitalist Class." *Science and Society* 64:1.

Ross, G. (1995) "Assessing the Delors Era and Social Policy." In S. Leibfried and P. Pierson, eds., *European Social Policy: Between Fragmentation and Integration.* Washington, D.C.: The Brookings Institution.

Ross, G. (2004) "Monetary Integration and the French Model." In A. Martin and G. Ross, eds., *Euros and Europeans: Monetary Integration and the European Model of Society.* Cambridge, UK: Cambridge University Press.

Roth, K. (2007) "Europe Must Pull Its Weight on Human Rights." *Financial Times.* January 12.

Ruggie, J. (1982) "International Regimes, Transactions, and Change: Embedded Liberalism in the Post-War Economic Order." *International Organization* 36:2.

Runciman, W. G. (1963) *Social Science and Political Theory.* Cambridge, UK: Cambridge University Press.

Ryner, M. (1998) "Maastricht Convergence in the Social and Christian Democratic Heartland." *International Journal of Political Economy* 28:2.

Ryner, M. (2002) *Capitalist Restructuring, Globalisation and the Third Way: Lessons from the Swedish Model.* London: Routledge.

Ryner, M. (2003) "Disciplinary Neoliberalism, Regionalization and the Social Market in German Restructuring." In A. Cafruny and M. Ryner, eds., *A Ruined Fortress? Neoliberal Hegemony and Transformation in Europe.* Lanham, Md.: Rowman & Littlefield.

Ryner, M., and T. Schulten. (2003) "The Political Economy of Labour Market Restructuring and Trade Unions in the Social Democratic Heartland." In H. Overbeek, ed., *The Political Economy of European Employment.* London: Routledge.

Sandholtz, W., and J. Zysman. (1989) "1989: Recasting the European Bargain." *World Politics* 42:1.

Sassen, S. (1991) *The Global City: New York, London, Tokyo.* Princeton, N.J.: Princeton University Press.

Scharpf, F. (1996) "Negative and Positive Integration in the Political Economy of European Welfare States." In G. Marks, F. Scharpf, P. Schmitter, and W. Streeck, eds., *Governance in the European Union.* London: Sage.

Schmid, J. (1998) "Wandel der Konsensstrukturen." In G. Simonis, ed., *Modell Deutschland nach der Wende.* Opladen, Germany: Leske & Budrich.

Schnabel, C., and J. Wagner. (2006) *The Persistent Decline in Unionization in Western and Eastern Germany, 1980–2004: What We Can Learn from a Decomposition Analysis.* IZA DP No. 2388. Nuremburg. October.

Schuldi, M. (2002) The Reform of Bismarckian Pension Systems. Ph.D. dissertation. Humboldt University of Berlin.

Seabrooke, L. (2001) *US Power in International Finance: The Victory of Dividends.* Basingstoke, UK: Palgrave Macmillan.

Seeleib-Kaiser, M. (2003) "Continuity or Change? Red-Green Social Policy After 16 Years of Christian-Democratic Rule." *ZeS-Arbeitspapier* 3. Bremen, Zentrum für Sozialpolitik.

Semmler, W. (1982) "Economic Aspects of Model Germany: A Comparison with the United States." In A. Markovits, ed., *The Political Economy of West Germany: Modell Deutschland.* New York: Praeger.

Servan-Schreiber, J-J. (1969) *The American Challenge.* New York: Atheneum.

Shonfield, A. (1965) *Modern Capitalism.* Oxford: Oxford University Press.

Siegel, N. (2004) "EMU and German Welfare Capitalism." In A. Martin and G. Ross, eds., *Euros and Europeans.* Cambridge, UK: Cambridge University Press.

Smith, A., A. Rainnie, and M. Dunford. (2001) "Regional Trajectories and Uneven Development in the 'New Europe': Rethinking Territorial Success and Inequality." In H. Wallace, ed., *Interlocking Dimensions of European Integration,* pp. 122–144. Basingstoke, UK: Palgrave Macmillan.

Solow, R. (2000) *Unemployment in the United States and Europe: A Contrast and the Reasons.* CESifo working paper 231. Munich. January.

Standing, G. (2003) *Global Labour Flexibility.* Basingstoke, UK: Palgrave Macmillan.

Stiglitz, J. (2002) *Globalization and Its Discontents.* New York: Norton.

Story, J., and I. Walter. (1997) *Political Economy of Financial Integration in Europe: The Battle of the Systems.* Cambridge, Mass.: MIT Press.

Strange, S. (1986) *Casino Capitalism.* London: Blackwell.

Streeck, W., and C. Trampusch. (2005) "Economic Reform and the Political Economy of the German Welfare State." Working paper 05/2. Max Planck Institut für Gesellschaftsforschung.

Talani, L. (2003) "The Political Economy of Exchange Rate Commitments: Italy, the United Kingdom, and the Process of European Monetary Integration." In A. Cafruny and M. Ryner, *A Ruined Fortress? Neoliberal Hegemony and Transformation in Europe.* Lanham, Md.: Rowman & Littlefield.

Talani, L. S. (2005) "The European Central Bank: Between Growth and Stability." *Comparative European Politics* 3:2.

Talani, L. S. (2006) "A Dead Stability Pact and a Strong Euro: There Must Be a Mistake." Paper presented at the International Studies Association Annual Convention, San Diego.

Tett, G. (2007) "Davos Rehearses Rivalry Between New York and London." *Financial Times.* January 26.

Therborn, G. (1980) *What Does the Ruling Class Do When It Rules?* London: Verso.

Therborn, G. (1987) "Welfare States and Capitalist Markets." *Acta Sociologica* 30:3/4.

Thornhill, J. (2005) "The Best and Worst of Times: Investors Look Beyond Europe's Political Malaise." *Financial Times.* December 28.

Tidow, S. (2003) "The Emergence of European Employment Policy as a Transnational Political Arena." In H. Overbeek, ed., *The Political Economy of European Employment.* London: Routledge.

Todd, I. (2002) *After the Empire: The Breakdown of the American Order.* New York: Columbia University Press.

Torfing, J. (1999) "Workfare Within Welfare: Recent Reforms of the Danish Welfare State." *Journal of European Social Policy* 9:1.

Trofimov, Y. (2003) "U.S. Army Camp in Kosovo Attracts Local Workers." *Wall Street Journal.* January 3.

Tsoukalis, L. (1997) *The New European Economy Revisited.* Oxford: Oxford University Press.

Twining, D. (2006) "America Is Pursuing a Grand Design in Asia." *Financial Times.* September 25.

Unger, R. M. (1976) *Law in Modern Society.* New York: Free Press.

United Kingdom HM Treasury. (2006) *The Case for Global Markets: How Increased Competition Can Equip Europe for Global Change.* HMSO, Office of Public Section Information. April.

United States Department of Defense. Office of the Undersecretary of State for Defense Policy. (2006) *Quadrennial Defense Review Report.* Washington, D.C.: DoD.

United States Treasury. Financial Management Service, Office of Macroeconomic Analysis. (2006) *Profile of the Economy.* Washington, D.C.: Dept. of Treasury. December.

Vail, M. (1999) "The Better Part of Valour: The Politics of French Welfare Reform." *Journal of European Social Policy* 9:4.

van Apeldoorn, B. (2002) *Transnational Capitalism and the Struggle over European Integration.* London: Routledge.

van Apeldoorn, B. (2006) "The Political Economy of European Integration in the Polder: Asymmetrical Supranational Economic Governance and the Limits of Legitimacy of Dutch EU Policy-Making." Research report commissioned by the Dutch Scientific Council for Government Policy, Amsterdam.

van der Pijl, K. (1984) *The Making of an Atlantic Ruling Class.* London: Verso.

van der Pijl, K. (1996) *Vordenker der Weltpolitik.* Opladen, Germany: Leske & Budrich.

van der Pijl, K. (1998) *Transnational Classes and International Relations.* London: Routledge.

van der Pijl, K. (2001) "From Gorbachev to Kosovo: Atlantic Rivalries and the Reincorporation of Eastern Europe." *Review of International Political Economy* 8:2.

van Kersbergen, K. (1995) *Social Capitalism: Study of Christian Democracy and the Welfare State.* London: Routledge.

Verdun, A. (1999) "The Role of the Delors Committee in the Creation of the EMU: An Epistemic Community?" *Journal of European Public Policy* 6:2.

Visser, J., and A. Hemerijck. (1997) *"A Dutch Miracle": Job Growth, Welfare Reform and Corporatism in the Netherlands.* Amsterdam: Amsterdam University Press.

Wade, R. (2003) "The Invisible Hand of the American Empire." *Ethics and International Affairs* 17:2.

Wallerstein, I. (2003) "Entering Global Anarchy." *New Left Review* 22.

Wall Street Journal. (2004) "As Jobs Head to Eastern Europe Unions in West Start to Bend." March 11.

Watson, M. (2001) "Embedding the 'New Economy' in Europe: A Study in the Institutional Specificities in Knowledge-Based Growth." *Economy and Society* 30:4.

Weisberg, J. (2006) "The Perils of Bush's Binge Borrowing." *Financial Times.* February 9.

Wighton, D., and B. White. (2007) "Wall Street Banks Cash in Overseas." *Financial Times.* January 21.

Wilensky, H. (1975) *The Welfare State and Equality: Structural and Ideological Roots of Public Expenditure.* Berkeley: University of California Press.

Wolf, M. (2005) "The Crushing Reality of Making the Eurozone Work." *Financial Times.* June 8.

Wylie, L. (2002) "EMU: A Neoliberal Construction." In A. Verdun, ed., *The Euro: European Integration Theory and Economic and Monetary Union.* Lanham, Md.: Rowman & Littlefield.

Zelikow, P., and C. Rice. (1995) *Germany Unified and Europe Transformed.* Cambridge: Harvard University Press.

Index

About the Book

EUROPE AT BAY IS A salvo in the debate about the prospects of the European Union and its role in the international arena. Challenging prevailing interpretations of EU politics, Cafruny and Ryner argue that current problems are not a result of integration per se, nor of the "growing pains" that are inevitable as governance gradually shifts from the nation-state to supranational institutions, but instead arise from more fundamental sources.

The authors eschew an idealized narrative as they explore the limits of the EU's economic and political power in relation to the United States, and of its neoliberal social and economic policies at home. They also consider the long-term prospects for the transatlantic relationship. Their work is a provocative contribution to a deeper and more comprehensive understanding of Europe's contemporary predicament.

Alan W. Cafruny is Henry Bristol Professor of International Affairs at Hamilton College. For several years a visiting professor at the European University Institute (Florence), he has also served as a member of the executive committee of the European Union Studies Association. His numerous publications include, most recently, *A Ruined Fortress? Neoliberal Hegemony and Transformation in Europe* (coedited with Magnus Ryner). **J. Magnus Ryner** is professor of international relations at Oxford Brookes University. He is author of *Capitalist Restructuring, Globalisation and the Third Way: Lessons from the Swedish Model* and coeditor of *Poverty and the Production of World Politics: Unprotected Workers in the Global Political Economy* and *A Ruined Fortress? Neoliberal Hegemony and Transformation in Europe*.